WOMEN IN THE FRONT LINE

Human rights violations against women

AI Index: ACT 77/01/91
ISBN: 0-939994-64-X
First published in March 1991
Amnesty International Publications
322 Eighth Avenue
New York, NY 10001

Published by John D. Lucas Printing, USA

This report reflects Amnesty International's information at the time of writing, December 1990.

Contents

1

Women in the front line

A pregnant woman detainee is punched in the stomach by police officers. An elderly woman is raped in front of her family by armed soldiers. A young girl is detained and sexually humiliated by government agents. A wife is tortured by interrogators to force her husband to "confess". A mother is shot dead by soldiers simply because her son is suspected of political activities. A daughter is threatened with death by government agents because she asks after her "disappeared" father.

The list of such gross human rights violations against women is endless. Many are targeted because they are strong — because they are political activists, community organizers, or persist in demanding that their rights or those of their relatives are respected. Others are targeted because they are seen as vulnerable — young women who can easily be sexually abused or humiliated, frightened mothers who will do anything to protect their children, pregnant women fearful for their unborn babies, women who can be used to get at men, or refugee women who are isolated and vulnerable in unfamiliar surroundings.

This report details human rights violations which are primarily suffered by women as well as a range of human rights abuses that women have experienced alongside men and children. By focusing on human rights violations committed against women, Amnesty International hopes to mobilize international support for the protection of women and, by extension, of all members of the societies in which they live.

This report records the experiences of women who have survived human rights violations. It also tells the stories of many who did not survive. The violations have occurred, and continue to occur, in every region of the world and under every system of government.

This is not a comprehensive account of all human rights violations against women, merely an indication of the type of atrocities women have suffered and therefore of what must be prevented from happening to anyone in the future. Nor is this a survey of all violations of women's human rights. It covers only those human rights violations which fall within Amnesty International's strictly defined mandate: to seek the release of prisoners of conscience — men and women detained solely for their beliefs, colour, sex, ethnic origin, language or religion, who have neither used nor advocated violence; to work for prompt and fair trials for all political prisoners; and to oppose the death penalty, extrajudicial executions and torture without reservation. Amnesty International covers a limited spectrum of rights, but not because it ignores the importance of other rights. It believes that there is a close relationship between all human rights but recognizes that it can achieve more by working within set limits.

Women's human rights, like those of men and children, are proclaimed in the Universal Declaration of Human Rights — the individual freedoms basic to human life. These include freedom of conscience, expression and association, freedom from arbitrary arrest and detention, freedom from torture, the right to a fair trial, and freedom from extrajudicial killing. These rights have been trampled on by governments around the world. However deep the economic, social or political crisis a government may face, there can never be a valid excuse for contravening fundamental human rights.

Women are primarily the victims of certain abuses. Rape, frequently used as a form of torture, is most often inflicted on women detainees. The United Nations (UN) Convention against Torture and Other Cruel, Inhuman or Degrading Treatment or Punishment prohibits "any act by which severe pain or suffering, whether physical or mental, is intentionally inflicted" for purposes such as obtaining information or punishing, intimidating, or coercing a person. No government agent should be permitted to commit or tolerate rape and other forms of sexual attack.

Women are particularly vulnerable to rape between the time of arrest and arrival at an official detention centre. Law enforcement officials have sometimes committed rape and other sexual abuse without officially arresting the victim. However, confinement in official detention centres does not necessarily protect women from rape or other sexual abuse.

For women who are pregnant at the time of detention, additional suffering often accompanies human rights abuses. They risk injury to the foetus, miscarriage or face the prospect of giving birth in harsh prison conditions. Women who become pregnant as a result of rape in custody face yet a further set of traumas.

Women are also subjected to cruel, inhuman or degrading treatment or punishment, including sexual humiliation, threats of rape and verbal abuses intended to degrade them. Women from all walks of life have been targeted for human rights abuse. In some cases, the reasons are connected with a woman's occupation or peaceful, legitimate activities. Governments detain or direct violent attacks against women who are physicians, lawyers, journalists, trade unionists, teachers, human rights activists, political activists, community organizers and members of many other professions. In other cases, women's human rights are violated because of their ethnic origin or religious beliefs.

Some women are subjected to human rights violations merely because they happen to be the wives, mothers, daughters or friends of people whom the authorities consider to be "dangerous" or "undesirable". These women are threatened, held as substitutes for their relatives, tortured or even killed as governments attempt to exert their will over those closely connected to them.

The leading human rights activists in many societies are prisoners' relatives: often wives and children, endlessly in the front line, campaigning for a prisoner's release, confronting government officials, trying to get information, trying to care for the prisoner. Prisoners' families bear the burden of providing assistance of all sorts — from daily meals, medicine and clothing, through to raising funds to pay legal fees, ransoms, or publicizing the case. In many African countries a strong tradition of family or community solidarity has protected prisoners in vulnerable situations. This has led some governments deliberately to exploit family relations, by imprisoning, threatening and harassing prisoners' relatives. In Guinea, under the rule of the late President Sekou Touré, wives were pressurized by the state to divorce their imprisoned husbands.

Countless women are forced to live in the shadow of another person's "disappearance". A woman may suddenly become her family's sole source of support just at the time when she is facing the absence of a close relative and is trying to locate the "disappeared" victim. She may be effectively widowed by her husband's "disappearance", yet unable to claim state or other benefits because her husband has not been declared dead, officially or legally. Members of the National Coordinating Committee of Widows of Guatemala have denounced their government's attitude to providing compensation. They have repeatedly alleged that government compensation is granted only if a widow attributes her husband's death to opposition guerrilla forces and if she ceases to pursue investigations into her husband's death or "disappearance".

Relatives of the "disappeared" face additional, emotional, suffering in many cultures. Women often refuse to give up hope, and search for years for husbands and children who have "disappeared", even though relatively few victims of "disappearance" survive this inhuman violation. But unless or until they reappear, or their bodies are found, their families suffer years of uncertainty, unable properly to mourn their loss and thus perhaps to lay their grief to rest.

In areas of civil turmoil or armed conflict, women are often subjected to brutal treatment simply because they live in a particular location or belong to a particular ethnic group. They are often caught in the crossfire between armed opposition groups and government forces, living under the threat of violence from both sides.

Amnesty International, as a matter of principle, condemns the torture and killing of prisoners by anyone, including opposition groups. It does not, however, treat such groups as though they had the status of governments. Nor does it address them unless they have certain of the essential attributes of a government, such as control over substantial territory and population. It is, after all, governments which have jurisdiction to determine criminal responsibility and to bring to justice those responsible for violent attacks on government authorities, security forces, and civilians. The state's exercise of such lawful authority, however, must conform to international standards of human rights and observe norms safeguarding fundamental human rights provided in domestic law.

Many governments do not uphold these norms. The rape of peasant women, either while in formal custody or when held by soldiers during counter-insurgency operations, is a common phenomenon in many countries. Governments often are complacent in the face of such abuses. Legal officials in Peru's Ayacucho department told Amnesty International representatives in 1986 that rape by government troops operating in rural areas was to be expected. In late September 1990, a Peruvian woman and her 17-year-old daughter were detained in a military base and repeatedly raped by a number of soldiers. Both women were subsequently released but warned not to report the rape. They have requested anonymity lest they suffer reprisals. Effective investigations into cases of rape in Peru are not known to have taken place, nor have the perpetrators been brought to justice.

Women refugees and asylum-seekers have also been the victims of sexual abuse by police, soldiers or other government agents. Many of these women lack the support systems which would be provided in their own communities or by their close relatives. With few resources to protect them from abuse or to provide means of redress, they become victims of a range of violations.

Cultural or social circumstances sometimes render women particularly isolated by the human rights violations they experience. They may choose not to report humiliating assaults by government agents because they fear this will result in reprisals from their own families, traumatic social repercussions, or further attacks by government officials.

Women who choose not to remain silent in the face of human rights violations inflicted upon them may face barriers such as official tolerance of the injuries caused to them. If they are from disadvantaged social or economic groups, they may find that official channels of communication are closed to them. Law enforcement officials may not listen, and the women may have nowhere to turn.

During the past decade, increasing numbers of women have spoken out for human rights protection. They have stated publicly and clearly what they and other members of their communities have suffered. They have also organized community and national groups to protest against human rights abuses. In some countries their vulnerability to such abuse has increased as they have assumed public leadership roles and spoken out about the special measures needed to protect women's human rights. Despite this, they continue to make their demands heard. The Committee of Mothers and Relatives of Political Prisoners, the Disappeared and the Assassinated, known as COMADRES, have been prominent for many years in the struggle to protect human rights in El Salvador. The COMADRES continue their work today, despite repeated threats against members of the group and violent attacks such as the October 1989 bombing of their offices.

The Mutual Support Group for the Appearance of Our Relatives Alive, known as GAM, has been a target of violence in Guatemala. GAM members press government authorities to account for those who "disappear". Several GAM leaders, including Rosario Godoy de Cuevas, were abducted and killed in 1985, apparently by government agents. Other GAM members are now the target of threats. The group's leader, Nineth Montenegro de García, has received so many death threats that human rights activists worldwide have sent appeals on her behalf to the Guatemalan authorities on several occasions.

Women have played prominent roles in South African human rights organizations such as the Detainees' Parents Support Committee and the Black Sash. Despite decades of repression, women activists have continued to mobilize against mass detentions, torture, and the injustices perpetuated by *apartheid*. Noma India Mfeketo attended the 1985 International Women's Congress in Nairobi, representing the United Women's Congress and the Federation of South African Women. Her international prominence, however, did not protect her when she returned home: she spent nine months in detention without charge or trial in 1987 and was again detained for several months in 1988 and 1989. Like many of her colleagues, she was detained solely for the peaceful exercise of basic human rights.

Susan Aniban of Task Force Detainees, a human rights group in the Philippines, was reportedly detained and tortured in November 1988. Numerous women human rights workers in the country have been subjected to such ill-treatment.

Several members of a women's organization were detained in Turkey in January 1990, after a police raid on the offices of the Association of Democratic Women in Ankara. They were reported to have been interrogated under torture.

The perseverance of women like these in the face of such persecution, along with the courage of many other women and men who continue to fight for human rights, has yielded significant results in recent years. The momentum to end patterns of abuse has increased as more women have joined efforts to publicize the facts and to press for change. More information than ever before is now available to the international community about what is happening to women worldwide. The international campaign is expanding and accelerating on behalf of women who struggled for their rights and did not survive, on behalf of women now struggling to survive, and on behalf not only of women but of all people who ought never to have to face human rights violations. The international human rights covenants, the UN Convention against Torture, the UN Convention on the Elimination of All Forms of Discrimination against Women, and many other agreements establish minimum standards of government responsibility. If governments ignore their responsibilities to any sector of society — whether to women, to men, to the young, or to members of ethnic or religious minorities — then no one's human rights are safe.

Safia Hashi Madar (right) was arrested in Somalia in 1985. She was nine months pregnant at the time, and gave birth the day after she was taken into custody. Her newborn son was taken away after the birth. She remained a prisoner of conscience for three and a half years.

Rosario Godoy de Cuevas (below) was abducted and killed in Guatemala in 1985. She was one of the leaders of a campaign to locate the "disappeared". Her husband, a trade union activist, had "disappeared" the year before.

Seviye Köprü (left), a Turkish nurse, was convicted and sentenced on the basis of a "confession" she made while in custody. In court she testified that she had "confessed" after being raped and beaten by police officers.

Fatima Abbas (left, below) has spent over four years in a Syrian prison because her husband was "wanted" by the authorities.

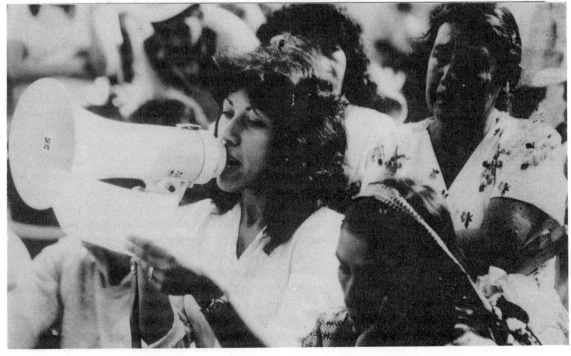

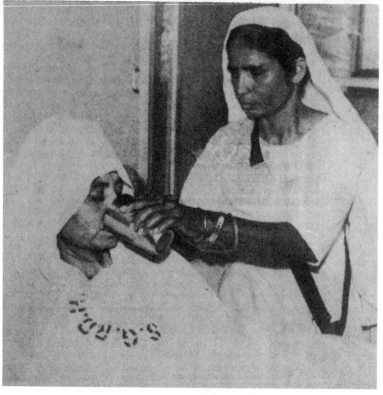

(Above) Wife and child of one of Peru's thousands of men who have "disappeared". Women are effectively widowed by "disappearance", yet are unable to claim state or other benefits because their husbands are not recognized to be legally dead. Many women have also "disappeared" in Peru.
(Right) Gurmeet Kaur, pictured in hospital, after a seven-day ordeal in the custody of the Indian police. She was reportedly detained and beaten because the authorities were trying to locate her husband.

(Above) Most of the world's refugees are women. Refugee women are often particularly vulnerable to human rights violations.

(Left) Gender is no protection against the most cruel, inhuman and degrading of human rights violations. Women have been executed in numerous countries during recent years. This photograph shows Samiha Abdel-Hamid, who was convicted of murder, moments before her 1987 execution in Cairo, Egypt

2

Victims from all walks of life

Women, no less than other members of society, are entitled to fundamental rights. Human rights treaties prohibit discrimination on the basis of sex in the protections they specify.

Governments deny women's basic human rights because of who the women are, what they have said or done, or where they happen to be. The victims of human rights violations include women of all ages and from all sectors of society.

Elba Julia Ramos was a cook at the Central American University and housekeeper for Jesuit priests who lived on the campus, located on the outskirts of El Salvador's capital city. During the early hours of a November morning in 1989, soldiers raided the campus and shot dead six of the priests. They then killed Julia Ramos and her 15-year-old daughter Celina Ramos, who were sleeping in their room near the priests' living quarters.

Local and international outrage over the killings eventually led to charges against nine members of the military, including a colonel accused of ordering the murders, but chain of command responsibility has still not been established. Official investigations of the case have proceeded slowly, however, largely due to the repeated lack of cooperation from the military.

Gönül Ortakçi, a Turkish housewife, was taken into custody in September 1987. On the basis of left-wing literature allegedly found in her possession, she was charged with membership of a political party declared illegal by the government and jailed. She was a prisoner of conscience for two months, held solely for the peaceful exercise of her basic rights, before being conditionally released in November 1987. The Izmir State Security Court acquitted her in November 1988.

Doina Cornea wrote an open letter to the Romanian authorities in August 1988, criticizing a plan by the Ceausescu government to destroy thousands of Romanian villages and to resettle the inhabitants in "agro-industrial" complexes. She continued to criticize government policies and the authorities placed her under virtual house arrest in November 1988. She was subjected to death threats and was assaulted by the police on several occasions before her confinement ended with the change of government in December 1989.

The Zairian authorities banished over a dozen women to remote areas of the country in 1988. The women had participated in a peaceful demonstration in the capital, Kinshasa, during April 1988 to protest against government policies which affected their work selling goods in urban markets. Officials apparently banished the women in order to deprive them of their livelihoods and to bar them from further political activities. Some of the women later returned to Kinshasa and were arrested and banished again in January 1989.

Information documented by Amnesty International in recent years indicates that women practising a broad range of occupations have been subjected to human rights abuses.

Medical personnel

Buthina Dowka, a nurse working at Khartoum Hospital, was among several hundred people arrested in Sudan's capital city following the military takeover in June 1989. The authorities held her for five months, although they never charged her with a criminal offence. She was apparently so severely ill-treated in custody that she suffered a mental breakdown.

Martha Angula was a Namibian midwife, practising her profession in the early 1980s for the South West African People's Organisation (SWAPO) in Angola, when she "disappeared". At the time, SWAPO was fighting against South African forces then occupying Namibia in defiance of UN resolutions. Martha Angula is believed to have left Namibia to join SWAPO and support its efforts to obtain Namibia's independence. But in 1985, she was arrested and confined in a SWAPO detention camp in Angola, apparently because she was suspected of spying. She was in her late 50s; according to another detainee in the camp, she became ill and was taken away, never to be seen again. Vicky Ashikoto, another midwife, then arrived at the camp, where a number of pregnant women were held. Detainees believed she had been arrested in order to replace Martha Angula as the camp midwife.

Teachers and students

Academics, especially those who are politically active, are targets of human rights violations in numerous countries. In China large numbers of students and academics were arrested in the wake of the government's crackdown on the pro-democracy movement in June 1989. Long Xianping, a 35-year-old teacher in Hunan province, spoke out publicly against the crackdown and participated in a protest against the killings by government troops. The authorities arrested her, charged her with "counter-revolutionary incitement", and sentenced her in December 1989 to two years' imprisonment.

The Turkish authorities detained Nurten Caglar, president of the student association at the Ankara University Law Faculty, in March 1989. She was taken to Ankara Police Headquarters and, according to reports, ill-treated. Five days before her arrest, a Turkish newspaper had alleged that leading members of the student association were affiliated to a youth organization deemed illegal under Turkish law. The authorities detained her for a week. The charges against her, if any, are not known.

The Somali authorities arrested Safia Hashi Madar, a biochemistry graduate who was working for an American relief organization in northwest Somalia, in July 1985, apparently because they suspected her of supporting an armed opposition group. She was nine months pregnant at the time of her arrest and went into labour the day afterwards. The authorities transferred her to hospital, where she underwent a complicated delivery. The next morning they returned her to prison, separating her from her newborn son and refusing to tell her for one week where they had taken him. She later learned that the infant had been handed over to his grandmother. Safia Hashi Madar was held for over three and a half years and released in March 1989. She was a prisoner of conscience.

Journalists

Journalists are among the women who face stiff penalties in some countries for exercising their right to free expression. Security police in Abu Dhabi in the United Arab Emirates arrested 29-year-old Dhabia Khemis Mehairi at her home in Sharjah in May 1987. She had helped to found a literary magazine in the United Kingdom, where she studied anthropology and literature. After returning to the United Arab Emirates in 1986, she had worked as a poet, writer, and television presenter. Her published articles reportedly addressed topics such as the status of Arab women in their societies. She was held without charge or trial for 10 weeks and then released. The authorities gave no reason for her detention. Her employers dismissed her from her post after her arrest.

Veliswa Mhlawuli was working as a journalist for a community-based newspaper in Cape Town, South Africa, when she was detained by security police in October 1988. She was held without charge for a time and then accused of offences under the Internal Security Act; she was released on bail in March 1989.

At the time of her detention, she was recovering

from the loss of an eye and other injuries inflicted by an unknown gunman. The assailant had attacked her shortly after the *British Broadcasting Corporation (BBC)* broadcast an interview with her in which she provided information about the alleged torture of children detained in South Africa. Before the attack, the authorities had publicly denied in their own television program the torture allegations made in the *BBC* film.

In a press interview, Veliswa Mhlawuli recalled the moments following the shooting. "I heard bones cracking, and my right cheek felt numb as I hit the ground. I lay there pretending I was dead, waiting for another bullet", she said. "My first thought was about the future of my two children. I thought I was dying." She was convicted in December 1989 of providing assistance to members of the then banned African National Congress and received a five-year suspended sentence.

In northeast India, Sanasam Ongbi Belu wrote an editorial criticizing the killings of alleged insurgents by Manipur state police. In October 1989, a week after her editorial appeared in a Manipuri journal, police arrested her for "favouring" the insurgents. The authorities subsequently charged her with sedition and "disruptive activities" and detained her for several days.

The Moroccan security forces raided the home of Embarca ment Taleb ould Husein at her home in the Western Sahara in September 1979, and took her away in a car. She was an announcer for "Radio Sahara" in Laayoune at the time. Well-read and independent, she was the first woman in the Western Sahara to obtain a driving licence. She has not been seen since her arrest.

Lawyers and judges
Solema Jubilan, a Filipino lawyer, provides free legal aid for political prisoners and disadvantaged people. She also operates a centre for orphans. In mid-1990 she was the target of a series of death threats. A staff attorney at her office in north Cotabato received five anonymous telephone calls in May, each from a different person and each threatening Solema Jubilan and her family with death. The evidence suggests that the threats came from government security forces attempting to curtail her legal work. Solema Jubilan had received such threats since 1986, when she arrived at work one day to find inscribed on her office door the words, "It would be nice to kill you".

Death threats also preceded the shotgun killing of María Elena Díaz Pérez, a Colombian judge, in July 1989. She had been investigating several mass killings of banana plantation workers when the threats began. María Elena Díaz had taken over the investigation from another woman judge, who left the country after receiving death threats. The investigation conducted by these judges linked army personnel to the mass killings. Unidentified gunmen carried out the killing of María Elena Díaz. Several other women judges investigating human rights violations attributed to military and paramilitary forces have received death threats. Some of them have left the country.

Political reformers
Women seeking political change in their countries have suffered a range of human rights violations. Aung San Suu Kyi returned in 1988 to Myanmar, formerly Burma, from the United Kingdom to care for her dying mother. The daughter of a nationalist hero, Aung San Suu Kyi soon acquired widespread popular support in her calls for reform. She became the leader of a new political party, the National League for Democracy (NLD), which then won a large majority of votes in the nationwide elections held in May 1990.

However, Myanmar's military rulers had disqualified Aung San Suu Kyi from standing in the election and placed her under house arrest in July 1989. Despite the NLD's election victory, the military government remained in power, and Aung San Suu Kyi remained under house arrest in late 1990.

Joana Simeao was one of many women involved in the struggle for Mozambique's independence from Portugal, but she was an opponent of the principal nationalist organization FRELIMO. She founded the opposition Mozambique Common Front, which promoted continuation of economic and political ties with Portugal, and was detained by FRELIMO forces when they assumed power. In April 1975, a few months before independence, she was among 24 prisoners paraded publicly at a FRELIMO camp in Tanzania, when FRELIMO leaders said they would not execute her or other members of rival groups. However, she and others subsequently "disappeared" in detention and are believed to have been killed.

Politically active Syrian women have also been arrested. Hind Qahwaji, an agricultural engineer, is among those detained for alleged membership of the Party for Communist Action, a political group declared illegal by the Syrian authorities. Officials first

Doina Cornea (above left) was placed under virtual house arrest because she criticized the policies of the Ceausescu government then in power in Romania.
Journalist Dhabia Khemis Mehairi (above right) was arrested in the United Arab Emirates after publishing an article on the issues facing women in Arab cultures.
Sara al-Fadil Mahmoud (right) was detained for three months in Sudan, after the government in which her husband was Prime Minister was overthrown in 1989.

arrested her in 1982, then released her in March 1983. Less than three weeks later, they again arrested her and held her under conditions which resulted in a serious deterioration of her health. A prisoner of conscience, she was still detained at the time of writing, December 1990. No formal charges had been brought against her and she had not been brought to trial.

In May 1989 Li Xiuping travelled from the Shenyang Medical University in China's Liaoning province to the capital, Beijing. She was a student and a leading member of the Autonomous Federation of Students from Outside Beijing and had gone to Beijing to participate in talks between student leaders and government representatives. As is well known, attempts to promote dialogue ended abruptly when government troops attacked and killed pro-democracy demonstrators in early June. The authorities arrested Li Xiuping on 18 June. She apparently remained in custody at the end of 1990.

Deborah Josephine "Debs" Marakalla was vice-president of the Tembisa Youth Congress in South Africa and a member of the Tembisa Detainees Support Committee when the authorities arrested her in July 1986. Her arrest was apparently connected with her community activities in Tembisa, a black township to the east of Johannesburg. She was held without charge or trial, a prisoner of conscience, until October 1987, when she was released under restriction orders. These were not lifted until February 1990. She was redetained under the state of emergency regulations on 12 April 1990 and released on 10 May without charge.

"Debs" Marakalla had become active in politics seven years earlier, while a schoolgirl in Tembisa. She was three months pregnant when she was arrested and miscarried in detention; she was denied adequate medical care and one of her fallopian tubes ruptured, with the result that doctors have told her that she can no longer bear children. She was 23 years old at the time of her arrest.

Women's rights activists

Women have also suffered human rights violations because of their work to protect women's rights.

"I was committed to the struggle for the liberation of women in Morocco", wrote Nezha Al Bernoussi in 1987 from her Moroccan prison cell. "Before my arrest I gave courses in reading and writing for illiterate women of all ages. These courses intended to teach the women reading and writing on the one hand; on the other, the courses were supposed to

awaken their sense for scientific progress."

In 1986, this 34-year-old woman, who may be a prisoner of conscience, received a six-year prison sentence on charges of conspiracy against the security of the state, membership of an illegal organization, and distribution of unauthorized leaflets. She was still serving her sentence in late 1990.

Amid civil turmoil in Peru, few men remain to carry on agricultural work in some areas of intense fighting. Women have responded to the economic crisis by establishing community kitchens, women's support networks, and groups to protect women's rights. This surge in activism has rendered women especially vulnerable to threats and attacks by the security forces.

Consuelo García Santa Cruz, a 26-year-old teacher and adviser on women's issues to the wives of workers in the Cerro de Pasco mines, was found dead in February 1989. Forensic reports indicate that her head had been crushed as if run over by a vehicle. Her body was discovered on the outskirts of the capital, Lima, near the body of a miners' union leader. The two appeared to have been extrajudicially executed.

Cecilia Olea, a Lima resident who belongs to the Flora Tristan women's group in Peru, received several death threats by telephone in the months preceding May 1989. Then in May she received a written threat signed by a paramilitary group reportedly linked to the armed forces. Flora Tristan members publicize women's issues through the mass media, organize educational programs, and provide legal and social assistance to working women. The author or authors of the written threat apparently considered Cecilia Olea's activities on behalf of women to be subversive and accused her of being a "communist".

The Israeli authorities arrested Tahani Sulayman Abu Daqqa in July 1988. She had organized a women's cooperative bakery and was active in the Palestinian Federation of Women's Action Committees in the Israeli Occupied Territories. The association offers medical, educational and economic assistance to Palestinian women and their children. The authorities held Tahani Sulayman Abu Daqqa for three months in administrative detention, without charge or trial, on account of her peaceful exercise of her rights to free association and free expression. According to reports, she was three months pregnant at the time of arrest and miscarried in detention.

María Cristina Gómez's body was found outside

El Salvador's capital city of San Salvador in early April 1989. The 41-year-old mother of four was a member of ANDES, a teachers' union, and a women's rights activist. Armed men abducted her on 5 April, in typical "death squad" style, at the school where she worked. An hour after the abduction her body was discovered, bearing gunshot wounds and indications that she may have been tortured. Just two weeks before her abduction, she had participated in the opening of a women's clinic, established to counsel victims of rape and battering.

Women involved in land conflicts
In many countries human rights violations occur in the context of land disputes. Many peasants and rural workers in Brazil have been harassed, threatened and killed as they attempt to defend their homesteads and communities from violent incursions by hired gunmen employed by large landowners and companies. The state authorities have persistently failed to bring those responsible to justice.

Some women have been killed in the context of land disputes. Gunmen shot dead Margarida Maria Alves, president of the Alagoa Grande rural workers' trade union in Paraíba state, in August 1983 as she stood on the front steps of her home. Lawyers investigating another "hired gun" killing found evidence that she had been killed by a death squad of civil and military police. A man charged with ordering the killing was not brought to trial until July 1988, and he was acquitted. A public prosecutor subsequently requested the reopening of inquiries into the case.

Maria Divina da Silva Santos, Sandra de Oliveira Souza, and 10 other homesteaders from Curionopolis, Pará state, were detained without warrant in July 1990. Police forced them to assist in locating male members of their community, threatening the detainees with summary execution if they failed to help in the search. The two women were held for three days, without charge, 200 kilometres from their home. Both women reportedly were beaten by police.

Members of religious faiths and organizations
Saudi Arabian authorities arrested Zahra' Habib Mansur al-Nasser, a housewife, in July 1989. As she and her husband returned from performing religious rites in Damascus border guards had searched them and found in Zahra al-Nasser's possession a Shi'a prayer book and a photograph of Ayatollah Kho-

meini. The majority of suspected government opponents arrested in the Eastern Province of Saudi Arabia during 1989 were Shi'a Muslims. Three days later her dead body, reportedly bearing marks of torture, was returned to her family.

Buddhist nuns in Lhasa, the capital of the Tibetan Autonomous Region of the People's Republic of China, have led several peaceful demonstrations since 1987 demanding independence for Tibet. In March 1988 four nuns who had demonstrated peacefully against Chinese rule were arrested, and reportedly stripped naked and beaten before being released without charge. Three of these nuns also reported sexual abuse. Another nun arrested in April 1988 was held without charge for three months. During her detention and interrogation about pro-independence activities, police are said to have set a dog on her which had been trained to attack.

Nineteen nuns from the Lhasa region were placed under administrative orders of "re-education through labour", without trial, in September and October 1989 for allegedly demonstrating in favour of Tibetan independence. The authorities reportedly tried 19-year-old Rinzen Choeny of the Shangsep convent for a similar offence in September 1989 and sentenced her to seven years' imprisonment.

Many church activists in El Salvador have suffered human rights violations. A woman church worker detained by the Salvadorian Treasury Police in November 1989 described the treatment she received in detention. She said that a rubber hood lined with lime had been placed over her head, she had been hung by her feet, and her head had been plunged into freezing water containing bits of ice. "There came a moment when I couldn't feel anything", she said. "Then they said, 'Confess, confess that you're a guerrilla'."

Relatives of male activists or prisoners
Some government authorities have detained, tortured, or killed women solely because of their family relationships or association with men considered to be "undesirable".

Following the June 1989 military coup in Sudan, the new authorities arrested some 80 government officials and other political leaders. In September 1989 the authorities arrested Sara al Fadil Mahmoud, wife of the former prime minister, and Sara Abdullahi Nugdullah, daughter of a former party official.

The women were held with convicted prisoners under harsh conditions for over one month, before being released without charge. Two days after their release, they were summoned by the authorities and instructed to sign incriminating statements. When the women refused to sign, they were immediately detained again. This time they were held for almost two months. Amnesty International considered both women to be prisoners of conscience.

Sri Lankan police took 16-year-old Gamaralalage Samanthilaka into custody in March 1988. Two of her brothers had been arrested previously, apparently on suspicion of belonging to an armed opposition group. The young woman's mother accompanied her into a police vehicle but was pushed out at the entrance to the police station, according to the teenager's testimony. In this she also described her interrogation about her brothers' associates and her denial of knowledge of their whereabouts. Her interrogators then assaulted her and forced her to watch them torture one of her brothers. Following her release, and in response to a legal action, the Sri Lankan Supreme Court in July 1990 instructed the authorities to compensate Gamaralalage Samanthilaka in July 1990 for having been arbitrarily arrested and tortured.

Over 70 Syrian women have been detained since 1987 apparently because of the alleged political activities of their male relatives. Most of them are reportedly still detained. Malika Khaluf, a nurse, was arrested at the same time as her brother. Asia al-Saleh, the mother of two children, one of them a five-month-old girl, was arrested with several of her relatives. It appears to have been the Syrian authorities' intention to force political suspects to renounce their political beliefs, by taking reprisals against their families.

Several other women were detained apparently to pressurize their male relatives to surrender to the authorities, although some of the women concerned then continued to be held after their male relatives gave themselves up.

Alita Bona was three months pregnant when Philippine soldiers detained her and her friend Soledad Mabilangan in March 1990 in the Philippines. The two women, both in their early twenties, were taken to a remote army camp high in the mountains of central Samar. The camp commander acknowledged to representatives of Amnesty International in mid-1990 that the women had not been charged with any offence. He said that Alita Bona and Soledad Mabilangan would be released if their husbands, allegedly members of a guerrilla group, "turned themselves in". The commander also said that the

two women had some freedom within the camp perimeter and were "allowed to cook for the soldiers". Army members encouraged the women held in secret detention to write to their husbands and urge them to surrender to the authorities.

In Guatemala Amnesty International has documented many cases in which government agents, or armed groups linked to them, have targeted women for persecution solely because of their relationship with alleged government opponents. For example, Consuelo Hernández Ramírez has continuously received death threats since her husband, a trade unionist, was murdered in 1989. Her husband, José Rolando Pantaleón, had worked for the Coca-Cola bottling plant in Guatemala City and had been a member of the trade union theatre group at the plant. The group had satirized the Guatemalan military in their skits. Men in plain clothes but wearing the type of jacket worn by police had often inquired about theatre group members' activities.

After her husband's death people dressed in civilian clothes came to Consuelo Hernández Ramírez' house several times, and asked where they could find her brother-in-law. They warned her that if she did not cooperate with them, she should think very carefully about her security and that of her children. She has reportedly said that although she is in danger, she does not want to leave the home she shared with her husband. She daily visits the cemetery where he is buried.

In Zaire Fatuma Mbholu and her son, Kahindo Bozelo, were arrested in March 1989 by government soldiers who apparently suspected the son of involvement in opposition activities. Fatuma Mbholu appears to have been detained for no other reason than to put pressure on her son. She was held in military custody but released after two weeks. Her son was also released without charge.

Fatima Oufkir, the widow of General Mohamed Oufkir, a Moroccan army officer allegedly involved in a 1972 coup attempt, has been detained without charge or trial for 18 years. She and her six children, along with a female cousin, are apparently detained solely because of their family ties with General Oufkir, who died in suspicious circumstances at the time of the coup attempt. They were held incommunicado and effectively "disappeared" until April 1987, when four of the children escaped and contacted lawyers to give news of their plight. Shortly after, they were rearrested. These eight relatives of General Oufkir, prisoners of conscience, were still detained at the end of 1990.

Other families have "disappeared" following their arrest by Moroccan forces in southern Morocco and the Western Sahara. It appears that they may have been targeted because a relative was suspected of sympathizing with the Polisario Front, an armed opposition group which advocates independence for the Western Sahara. Eleven members of the family of Mohamed Lamine ould Ahmed have been arrested by Moroccan security forces since 1976 and are said to have "disappeared". They include his sister, Fatma Ghalia, his mother, Mainouna ment Abdallahi, and an aunt, Tagla Mohamed Abdallahi Ould el-Hassan el-Leili.

In Turkey, Ramazan Velieceoglu testified in court in December 1988 that he had "confessed" to membership of an illegal organization because the police had detained his wife. Before that, he said, he had been interrogated, beaten and tortured with electric shocks for seven days. He agreed to "confess" when his wife was detained and threatened with torture.

In the Philippines and Senegal, as in numerous other countries, neither tender nor advanced age offers any protection against violations of the most fundamental human rights.

In the Philippines, the bodies of Hugo Paner's 14-year-old daughter, Rosie, and her friend Edna Velez, aged 16, were discovered in April 1987. Witnesses reported that more than 60 government soldiers had surrounded the Paner home, apparently because they suspected Hugo Paner of involvement in armed opposition to the government. But he was not at home, so the soldiers took the girls instead. They took them outside the house. Witnesses then heard screams. Afterwards, the two girls' bodies were found with multiple stab wounds and there was evidence of sexual assault.

In Senegal, a 60-year-old woman held in Rufisque prison told representatives of Amnesty International in 1985 that she had been detained incommunicado for over 18 months for allegedly participating in a demonstration. She said that police had stripped her naked and beaten her with batons. Another woman, aged about 65, who was held at the same prison said she had been arrested while walking to a holy site, for reasons which are still unclear.

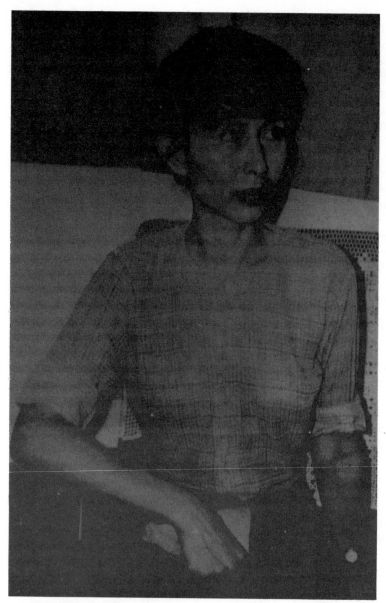

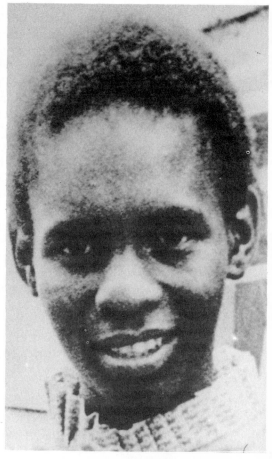

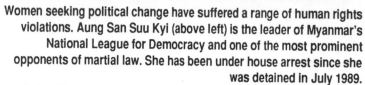

Women seeking political change have suffered a range of human rights violations. Aung San Suu Kyi (above left) is the leader of Myanmar's National League for Democracy and one of the most prominent opponents of martial law. She has been under house arrest since she was detained in July 1989.

"Debs" Marakalla (above right), Vice-President of the Tembisa Youth Congress in South Africa, was pregnant when she was detained and held without charge or trial for over a year because of her community activities. She miscarried while in custody and was denied adequate medical care.

Zahra' Habib Mansur al-Nasser (right) died in custody in a Saudi Arabia border checkpoint, allegedly as a result of torture. She was arrested in July 1989 as she returned from Damascus, where she had gone to perform Shi'a Muslim religious rites.

Fatima Oufkir (left), widow of a Moroccan army general allegedly involved in a 1972 coup attempt, has been detained with her six children and another relative for almost 18 years. She and her children have not been charged or tried. They were held incommunicado until 1987. Dona Maria da Guia (below), leading member of a Brazilian rural workers' union, received death threats because of her trade union activities.

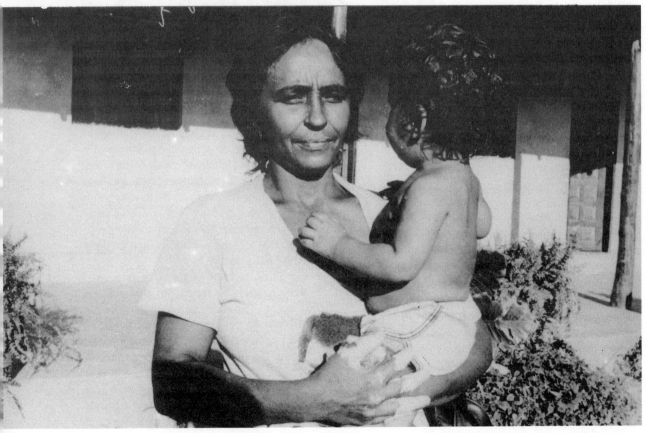

3

The human rights abuses women suffer

Governments around the world have not limited their cruel and degrading practices to women. Some types of human rights violations, however, are particularly directed against women, and affect them in especially severe ways. Pregnant women who are tortured, or who are held in inhuman conditions, face unique horrors; they may suffer miscarriages or sustain permanent injury to their reproductive organs as a result. Women are subject to special forms of sexual abuse, with rape in particular being used to inflict severe, and often long-term, physical and psychological injury. Women who were raped in custody by government agents have become pregnant as a result, with all the added trauma that this can induce.

Although, clearly, women victims of human rights violations may suffer common experiences, each individual's suffering is also unique. However, a woman's sex, as well as her role within a family and her cultural environment, may influence the way in which her human rights are abused by governments.

Rape

In some countries rape by government agents is a common method of torture inflicted on women detainees. It is both a physical violation and injury, and an assault on a woman's mental and emotional well-being. Interrogators and other government officials have used rape as a form of torture in attempts to intimidate women from pursuing particular activities and to extract information or "confessions" from them.

Rape constitutes an especially humiliating assault. Consequently, it often carries traumatic social repercussions, which may be affected by a woman's cultural origins or social status. Such factors may affect her ability to bear the trauma of rape, let alone the time it may take for her to come to terms with the emotional distress and physical effects of rape. All government agents who rape, or encourage or condone the rape of, individuals in their custody should be brought to justice.

In some countries women who have been raped in custody are unwilling to report the abuse. Some women, it seems, feel they must obliterate the experience from their memory; others feel degraded and ashamed or fear that they would suffer social stigma should they disclose what has been done to them. In some countries, moreover, a woman who has been raped, even though it was by a government agent while she was defenceless, may face reprisals from her relatives. A common accompaniment to rape is a perpetrator's threat of additional violence if the victim tells anyone of the assault.

In El Salvador testimonies indicate that rape has been commonly used as a form of torture in attempts to extract information from women detainees and to intimidate into ceasing activities viewed as "subversive". María Juana Medina was one of 64 people arrested in September 1989 during a demonstration protesting against recent detentions and abductions of trade unionists. Her daughter, Sara Cristina Chan-Chan Medina, had worked as a photo-journalist for the major Salvadorian trade union federation FENAS-TRAS and "disappeared" after being arrested in August 1989.

María Juana Medina testified in November 1989, after her release, that she and others were beaten by police at the National Police headquarters. Their foreheads were then marked with numbers and they were summoned individually for interrogation. María Juana Medina reported: "When my turn came to be interrogated, I was taken to a room. A man took off my clothes and began to question me. He made me lie on the floor and told me to remove my underwear. I said no. He took it off and raped me". She was again tortured, she said, when she repeatedly denied any connection with the trade union federation other than through her efforts to locate her daughter. The next day a doctor in the detention centre examined her injuries and recommended that she be immediately taken to hospital. Concluding the description of her experience, María Juana Medina said, "I was made to sign a piece of paper while I was blindfolded. I do not know what the paper said".

In India, the judiciary has on occasions expressed concern about official inaction in relation to cases of rape in custody. The Supreme Court of India noted in 1987 what it called the "pathetic state of affairs" in Gujarat state, where the state government had failed to act on the findings of a court-appointed commission of inquiry into one rape case.

The rape of women prisoners by Indian police has been widely documented. In the late 1980s, official records indicate that about 1,000 cases of alleged rape were annually reported by women belonging to the disadvantaged sectors of society known as Scheduled Castes and Tribes. Many of these 1,000 rapes were reportedly committed by police who held the women in custody for a variety of reasons. Often, it seems, allegations of the rape of women prisoners are not investigated and police officers accused of committing rape are rarely convicted.

Such investigations as do occur are often conducted by the police themselves, rather than independent bodies, with medical examinations of alleged victims being carried out by police doctors or other government physicians, whose impartiality may be in question.

In one case in Gujarat state police took 22-year-old Gunta Behn from her house in January 1986 in connection with their investigation into the abduction of one of her relatives. They reportedly stripped her naked before a crowd in her village before putting her in a police truck where, she said, she was raped by four policemen. Afterwards, she alleged that they took her to the Sagbara town police station and again raped and assaulted her. In addition, an officer reportedly inserted a bamboo rod inside her vagina, causing profuse bleeding. Two days later she was taken to the Rajpipla police station, where doctors apparently refused to examine her without orders from the chief of police. She was later released and consulted a private doctor. An official investigation into her case found that eight people — police officers, local officials, and doctors — had participated in the rape or in attempting to cover it up. However, none of them had been brought to trial by late 1990 for raping Gunta Behn.

In another case, police allegedly raped 20 women at Pararia village, in India's Bihar state, in February 1988. The police are said to have raided the village after a dispute arose between a villager and a police officer, and to have beaten and detained many of its male residents as well as raping the women. Subsequently, 14 police officers were suspended from duty, and 10 were arrested for the assaults.

A *Times of India* editorial noted in 1986, "Custodial rapes seem to be occurring so frequently that 'cop molests woman' has become an almost daily fare for newspaper readers. Considering that as many as 97 per cent of rape cases are either cancelled or sent back as 'untraced' by the police according to its own admission, the difficulties in dealing with custodial rape cannot be underestimated".

Legislation promulgated in India in September 1989 seeks to protect members of the Scheduled Castes and Tribes, recognized as especially vulnerable, from such assaults. Evidence compiled in 1990, however, indicates that rape by police and paramilitary forces continued to be widespread, especially in the state of Jammu and Kashmir.

Rape in police custody is regularly reported in Pakistan. Two women alleged in July 1989 that Punjab provincial police beat them with leather thongs and that at least six police officers raped them and also thrust sticks into their vaginas. A 16-year-old criminal suspect in Sind province reported that police raped her and forced chillies into her vagina. As a protective measure, a High Court judge said in July 1989 that women should be detained only in judicial, and not in police, custody.

Cases of women raped in custody were also reported in Romania prior to the December 1989 change of government. Police detained Ana Ciherean in October 1989 apparently because she had expressed a desire to leave the country and later had met with a foreign acquaintance. Her dead body was found in a park the day after her detention. Details of her treatment in custody are not known. However, her body showed evidence of rape, and her arms and legs had been broken.

The authorities in Myanmar, formerly Burma, have used rape as a punitive measure. In June 1986, when government soldiers saw an 11-year-old girl and her 22-year-old aunt attempting to return to their homes, after an officially declared curfew, they reportedly took them into custody and raped them. An eyewitness said that the two were compelled "to spend the night with the soldiers. The older one was raped by six soldiers, while her niece was first raped twice by the unit commander and then by seven soldiers taking turns". In another case, a 30-year-old woman, detained by Myanmar soldiers in November 1986, witnessed the rape by an army major of another woman in custody, apparently to punish the victim for involvement in trading practices prohibited by the military as part of their counter-insurgency operations. The witness said: "I saw him raping her before my eyes. She cried, but because she was beaten, she did not dare to cry any longer".

Military personnel operating in areas of armed insurgency are often given broad powers and not held to account for their actions. Peru provides one such example. In 1986 officials there told an Amnesty International delegation visiting the department of Ayacucho that rape was to be expected when troops were based in rural areas and that prosecutions for such assaults should not be anticipated.

In the light of this, it is scarcely surprising that women in Peru's emergency zones are alleged to have been widely subjected to rape and other abuse by soldiers who are able to act with impunity. On many occasions soldiers are reported to have entered villages, rounded up the residents, separated men

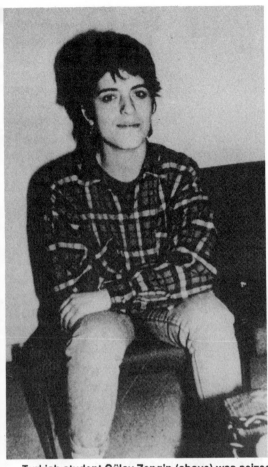

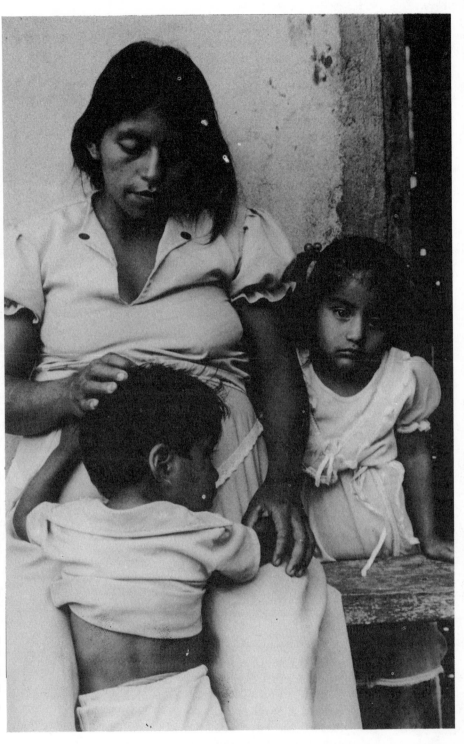

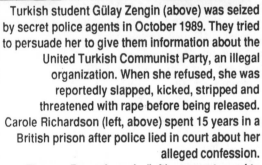

Turkish student Gülay Zengin (above) was seized by secret police agents in October 1989. They tried to persuade her to give them information about the United Turkish Communist Party, an illegal organization. When she refused, she was reportedly slapped, kicked, stripped and threatened with rape before being released.
Carole Richardson (left, above) spent 15 years in a British prison after police lied in court about her alleged confession.
Theresa Ramashamole (left) was sentenced to death in South Africa in 1985. In 1988 she and her five co-defendants, known as the "Sharpeville Six", had their sentences commuted to long terms of imprisonment.

The family of Indian leader César Aquite, victim of a "death squad" in Colombia.

from women, and then raped the women. On other occasions, women have been raped by soldiers in their homes or during interrogation in secret detention centres. However, to date no army personnel stationed in Peru's emergency zones are known to have been prosecuted for rape, and no effective investigations into complaints of rape by soldiers are known to have occurred.

One alleged victim was María Guinarita Pisco Pisango. She lived in the San Martin de Alao community of Peru's San Martin department. In January 1988, she travelled to the departmental capital in search of information about her husband, who had "disappeared" earlier that month. While in the capital, she reported his "disappearance" to the local human rights commission of San Martin Department. Following this, at midnight on 17 January, soldiers burst into her home where she lived with her parents and three children. The soldiers tied up her elderly parents and abducted María Guinarita Pisco. Her body was found on 19 January; her hands were tied behind her back, she was still blindfold, and she had been shot in the forehead. It also appeared that she had been raped, and tortured in other ways, before she was killed.

A woman teacher who was detained for several days at a small army post in the Abancay department of Peru alleged that she was stripped naked, suspended from a rope, slashed with a knife, and repeatedly raped. She was set free after school officials pressed for her release, but she was apparently threatened that she would be killed if she told anyone of her treatment in detention. Further details of her case have been omitted for her protection.

Rape sometimes appears to be used as a form of torture because those responsible realize that their victims may be constrained from revealing what has occurred after their release from custody. The shame associated with rape can be a strong inducement to silence. In Colombia a woman who testified in March 1990 that military personnel had raped her in custody said that they had told her "to forget everything because my dignity as a woman was compromised, and my husband was not going to like knowing this". She was released only after agreeing to sign a statement declaring that she had been treated well in custody. She now lives in exile.

Another woman, released from Iran's Evin Prison, reported that a woman imprisoned with her for political reasons could not cope with the rape and other assaults committed by prison guards. The former prisoner said, "Rafat Kholdi was raped... She lost her

mental balance but was not given care and needed treatment. Her condition worsened, and she finally killed herself in prison in November 1988."

There is evidence to suggest that the rape of women in custody may often go unreported or undetected. Even so, enough information is available to indicate that rape of women prisoners by police, soldiers and guards has been widespread throughout the last decade. Rape can often be used as an instrument of political repression. And the victim's suffering can endure for the rest of her life.

Sexual humiliation, threats, and other abuse

Sexual abuse of women in custody by government authorities takes many forms in addition to rape: sexual contact falling short of rape, verbal humiliation, threats of violent attack, or forced acts intended to degrade a woman. These abuses may take place in an interrogation cell, in a room at a police station, in a prison cell, in a back alley, or at an isolated rural site. They may also occur in public, in the presence of a woman's family or neighbours. By subjecting women in their custody to sexual abuse, government agents may seek to intimidate entire sectors of the population.

A former prisoner has described at length her experiences in Somalia's Hargeisa Central Prison. Women guarding the prisoners, she said, often allowed male soldiers stationed at the prison gates to "visit" the female prisoners in order to fondle them or make other sexual advances towards them. Women prisoners who resisted such "visits" reportedly risked severe punishment, including permanent injury from a vice-like instrument placed around the foot and screwed together so tightly that it crushed the foot.

Former detainees in Somalia have also reported that guards punished them for complaining about harsh prison conditions by taking away their clothes. Some women, they said, were made to lie naked and handcuffed in the prison courtyard in full view of soldiers and male prisoners. In another incident at Hargeisa Central Prison, the prison authorities reportedly punished a group of women for singing by stripping them naked and then subjecting them to "inspection" by the prison commander; he subsequently ordered them to march, still naked, into the men's section of the prison where he "offered" them to male prisoners.

In a number of cases, Muslim women freed from political imprisonment in Pakistan are said to have been reluctant to state publicly, or even to tell close relatives, the details of their treatment in detention. However, some have described their experiences. A woman arrested in Pakistan for alleged political activities in 1983 spoke after her release about the treatment she underwent at Lahore Fort, a military detention centre. Guards continually subjected her to severe verbal abuse and verbal humiliation, she said, and she found these forms of abuse more difficult to bear than the physical abuse she experienced.

In the Israeli Occupied Territories, Palestinian women have accused Israeli security forces of subjecting them to sexual humiliation — fondling, threats of sexual violence, degrading verbal abuse and, in some cases, ill-treatment that could affect their pregnancies. Rula Abu Dahu, a Palestinian woman who was arrested by Israeli security forces in February 1988 and later sentenced to 25 years' imprisonment for participating in a murder, alleged in a sworn statement that she had been abused. She said that soldiers entered her home without a warrant at about 2am and took her to a Jerusalem detention centre known as the Russian Compound. She alleged that the soldiers hit her with their rifles and verbally abused her with sexual innuendo during the journey and that a male interrogator at the detention centre told her that he wanted to rape her. "I will take your breast and put it on the table and punch it", he reportedly said to her. "I will make sure that you will not be able to be a woman any more." She said that only men were present while she was being interrogated, although according to Israeli practice a woman is usually present during the interrogation of a woman prisoner.

In another case, a Palestinian woman charged with weapons offences by the Israeli authorities testified in a sworn statement that her interrogators sexually abused her in their attempts to force a "confession" from her in November 1986. Fatma Abu Bakra alleged that when she was alone with one male interrogator, who "played with my face and my breasts" and repeatedly said that he wanted to engage in sexual acts with her. After handcuffing her and forcing her to sit on the floor, she continued, he "sat with his legs open on a chair in such a way that I had to sit between his legs." She said he continued to fondle her, and that when she threatened to report his actions, he replied that he did not care about "public opinion, lawyers, or the Red Cross". Fatma Abu Bakra concluded her testimony, given to a woman lawyer, by saying: "I was too embarrassed to give details of this event to the male lawyers from Gaza who came to visit me, and I still feel embarrassed".

Elisa "Tita" Lubi was arrested in the Philippines in June 1988 by government troops and charged with "subversion". A medical report substantiates her claim that she was sexually molested by soldiers while detained. She was also subjected to other forms of ill-treatment and denied her right to contact a lawyer and members of her family. After repeated postponements of her arraignment, the court finally dismissed her case for lack of evidence, over six months after her arrest.

Threats of rape have been widely reported by women held in Turkish police stations. Police officers have reportedly stripped women detainees, sometimes in the presence of their relatives or associates, and tortured them. Solmaz Karabulut, who was arrested in March 1989 at the school where she taught, said that police officers in Ankara, who accused her of belonging to an illegal opposition organization, beat her, stripped her naked, threatened her with rape, and tortured her with electric shocks.

A woman arrested in Chad in 1987, possibly because she had made inquiries about her husband and son, who were imprisoned and believed killed in 1986 or 1987, said she was taken with 10 other women prisoners to a military post in northeast Chad. She said they were forced to do hard labour at the barracks there and soldiers forced the young women among them to perform as prostitutes. The women were then subjected to similar treatment at a second barracks. None of the women had been tried or sentenced.

A 19-year-old Austrian woman lodged a formal complaint in mid-1990 about sexual acts forced upon her at the Karlsplatz police post in Vienna. Two police officers detained the young woman in May 1990, according to press reports. She said that the two officers forced her to have oral sex with them at the police post and gave her drugs, in the form of tablets, as a "reward". A third officer reportedly knew that the sexual assault was taking place but failed to intervene. The woman, whose identity has been withheld to protect her privacy, was homeless at the time of her detention. According to reports, the two police officers who assaulted her have been suspended from duty, and the officer who failed to intervene faces disciplinary charges.

Misuse of prison regulations can also constitute cruel or degrading treatment. Strip-searching conducted with the deliberate intention of humiliating the prisoner is one example of such abuse. During 1986 guards in the United Kingdom's Brixton

Prison strip-searched two women prisoners virtually every day, and sometimes up to three times daily. Amnesty International received allegations that these strip-searches were a wilful attempt to humiliate the women.

Women held in Armagh Prison in Northern Ireland reported during the 1980s that as many as four women prison guards were sometimes present during strip-searches. Amnesty International was concerned about allegations that strip-searches of women prisoners in Armagh Prison in recent years had not been carried out solely for security purposes, but with the deliberate intention of degrading or humiliating the women. Amnesty International urged the government to reconsider its policy on strip-searching.

Pregnancy and human rights abuse

The special needs of pregnant women are recognized in international instruments such as the UN Standard Minimum Rules for the Treatment of Prisoners and Protocol I to the 1949 Geneva Conventions. Some governments not only ignore these special needs but sometimes take advantage of the special vulnerability of pregnant women to inflict severe physical and emotional pain.

A pregnant woman is particularly vulnerable to torture or to detention in cruel and degrading conditions. She risks miscarriage in such circumstances and severe injury from untreated medical complications of pregnancy. She also risks bearing an injured child, and faces the prospect of separation from her newborn infant, if the authorities decide to remove the child, or of attempting to raise a child in prison. A woman who becomes pregnant in detention as a result of rape faces additional emotional distress.

Wafa' Murtada was a 27-year-old civil engineer and nearly nine months pregnant when the Syrian authorities arrested her in September 1987. The authorities apparently suspected her husband of belonging to a banned opposition group and tried to extract the names of his associates from her. After being tortured Wafa' Murtada gave birth prematurely in prison. She reportedly remained in detention without charge or trial in late 1990.

After Na'ila 'A'esh was arrested in the Israeli Occupied Territories during February 1987, the authorities reportedly hooded her, knocked her head against a wall, and forced her to stand in bitterly cold conditions for prolonged periods. She was in the early stages of pregnancy, according to reports, and when the authorities denied her access to medical attention for bleeding, she miscarried. Palestinian women held at Ha Sharon Prison in Israel reportedly began a hunger-strike in April 1990 to demand improved prison conditions, especially for pregnant women.

In Brazil teenage prostitutes working in Recife are reported to have miscarried after military police detained them on the streets, kicked and beat them.

Kim Young-ae was working for an opposition newspaper in South Korea when the police arrested her and her husband in August 1989. She was charged under the National Security Law with passing opposition publications to "anti-state" organizations in Europe and was brought to trial in December 1989. She testified in court that she had miscarried as a result of the beatings she received in pre-trial detention. She received a seven-year prison sentence, and Amnesty International considered her to be a prisoner of conscience. Following a High Court appeal of her case, she was freed on bail in mid-June 1990.

In Chile Patricia Peña testified that she became pregnant after being raped in custody. Members of the state security police arrested the 19-year-old woman during a demonstration against government policies in September 1986. After her release on bail in January 1988, she testified that interrogators at a detention centre had tortured her with electric shocks and raped her. They later forced her to sign a statement, without allowing her to read it, and confined her to prison. While she was in prison, Patricia Peña realized that she was pregnant as a result of the rape. She began to experience severe pain and bleeding but there were reportedly long delays before she received adequate medical attention. She miscarried in late November 1986.

Reports from India also describe abuses against pregnant women. During 1987 counter-insurgency operations conducted by Assam Rifles troops in Manipur state, troops detained entire populations of villages. Soldiers held all of the villagers in the open air or in churches for 12 hours daily, week after week. They made no exceptions for pregnant women, according to reports. Pregnant women living in some villages were also subjected to beatings. At least two women reportedly miscarried shortly after soldiers had beaten them.

Torture, ill-treatment and other abuses

In addition to those abuses to which their sex makes them particularly vulnerable, women also suffer forms of torture, ill-treatment and harassment which are not gender-specific.

After her release from detention in March 1989, 19-year-old Sophie Mahlaela described the brutality to which South African police had subjected her. She alleged that they had placed a sack over her head, administered electric shocks to her head, back, and the soles of her feet, thrown her against a wall, and forced her to perform physical exercises for prolonged periods.

Ana Tsambasis was among a group of students allegedly tortured by Greek police officers in June 1986. She was arrested after a demonstration at the Aristotle University of Thessaloniki, during which two policemen were seriously injured. Ana Tsambasis said that policemen threw her against a wall, shouted at her, and pulled her hair. Groups of interrogators questioned her about individuals suspected of involvement in the demonstration. The physical abuse alternated with interrogation for over 24 hours, she said.

Women who play a prominent role in their communities have often received death threats. A Colombian woman received such threats in mid-1990. Elvia Urán de Beltrán works for a human rights organization in Medellín, Colombia. A caller reportedly told her in July that if she continued her work on behalf of political prisoners she would suffer the same fate as Dr Alirio de Jesús Pedraza Becerra. He had "disappeared" less than a week earlier, after heavily armed men believed to be members of the security forces took him into custody.

An unidentified man reportedly threatened a leader of the human rights movement in Peru's Ayacucho department in August 1988. He burst into Angélica Mendoza de Ascarza's office and told her that if she did not stop the work she was doing, she would "disappear" or die. Angélica Mendoza de Ascarza is the president of a national association which works on behalf of the "disappeared" in Peru's emergency zone. Members of the Peruvian Intelligence Police raided her home, allegedly seeking people unknown to her, about six weeks after the incident in her office.

A number of Palestinians, who were especially vulnerable because of their age or state of health, were victims of the apparently deliberate misuse of tear-gas in the Israeli Occupied Territories during the late 1980s. Members of the Israeli Defence Forces fired tear-gas canisters into buildings and other confined spaces where they could result in lethal injury. Amal 'Abd al-Wahad Qasisa, a five-day-old baby, died in her crib after soldiers fired

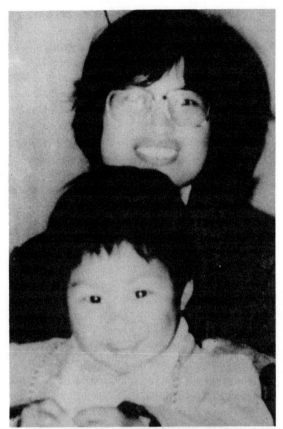

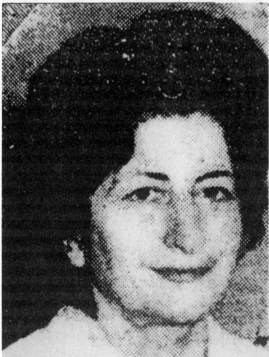

Prisoners of conscience: Long Xiangping (top) is serving a two-year sentence in China. Miriam Firouz (above) imprisoned in Iran since 1983.

In 1988 school student Nafige Zendeli (above left) was sentenced to four years' imprisonment in Yugoslavia. She was 18 years old. Nonyamezelo Victoria Mxenge (above right) was shot dead by four unidentified gunmen, possibly linked to the security forces, in August 1985 in South Africa. At the time she was defending 16 leading members of the United Democratic Front. Husniyya 'Abd al-Qader (right) organizes kindergartens and sewing workshops in Balata refugee camp in the Israeli-occupied West Bank. She has twice been placed under administrative detention.

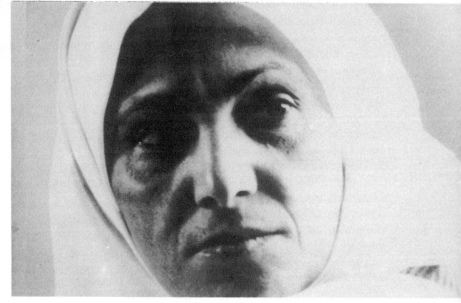

tear-gas directly into her house. Wijdan Faris, a woman in her final month of pregnancy, was baking bread in a small room which opened onto a courtyard when a number of tear-gas canisters were fired into the yard. She collapsed and was taken to hospital, where she died shortly after arrival.

Reports that political prisoners were subjected to drug misuse have been received from the Soviet Union, most frequently before the advent of the government's recent policy of "openness and restructuring".

Anna Chertkova was confined in a psychiatric hospital for over a decade because she had refused to renounce her religious convictions. Reports that hospital personnel had repeatedly injected her with the powerful drug Sulfazin emerged in the early 1980s. She was released from custody in December 1987.

The Turkish authorities reportedly detained Berrin Ceylan, whom they suspected of belonging to an illegal organization, in total darkness for seven days in 1989. Throughout this period she heard the screams of other detainees undergoing torture.

Martina Shanahan was subjected to prolonged isolation by the United Kingdom authorities. They arrested her and two men in August 1987. Unlike her co-defendants, Martina Shanahan was isolated from all other members of the prison population for over 200 days preceding her trial on charges of conspiracy to murder. At her trial, her lawyer noted that even convicted prisoners who break prison rules may be deprived of association with other prisoners for only 55 days. Until her case came to trial Martina Shanahan was allowed only one weekly visit from her family, lasting from 15 to 30 minutes. A psychiatrist who examined her reported that she had suffered serious impairment of her mental functions during her prolonged isolation.

For most of the past seven years Phyllis Coard has been held in solitary confinement at Grenada's Richmond Hill Prison. United States troops arrested her in 1983, following the invasion of Grenada, and transferred her to Grenadian custody shortly after her arrest. She is one of 14 people sentenced to death in October 1983 for the murder of Prime Minister Maurice Bishop and others. Unlike other prisoners condemned to death in Grenada, Phyllis Coard has been denied contact with other prisoners. She has been periodically denied visits from relatives and friends, sometimes for several months. She reportedly received no visits between February and July

1990. Correspondence, including letters from her children, has also been withheld from her.

Exploitation of family relationships

The authorities in some countries have exploited family relationships to intensify torture and ill-treatment. A woman's husband or children may be tortured in her presence, or a woman may be tortured to increase the suffering of her imprisoned spouse, son or daughter. These gross human rights violations or threats of such violations combine assault on individual dignity with assault on family integrity.

Fatma Özyurt, a Turkish worker, was detained in March 1989 and interrogated for over 20 days at Ankara Police Headquarters. In a formal complaint, she said that her interrogators stripped her naked, hosed her with cold water, suspended her by her arms, beat her, gave her electric shocks and sexually assaulted her, in an attempt to force her to "confess" to membership of an illegal organization. She said that she was forced to witness the torture of her sisters, Arife and Nahide, from whom the police were also trying to extract "confessions".

Syrian authorities have also exploited family relationships in attempts to extract confessions. A political prisoner released in 1985 stated that the authorities detained his mother and threatened to torture her, along with his father, if he refused to sign a confession.

A two-year-old Guatemalan child and his mother were surrounded by four armed men in July 1989. The men reportedly held guns to the child's head and threatened to kill him if his mother, Ana Graciela del Valle, failed to deliver a warning to her brother-in-law, the director of a Guatemalan human rights group. The assailants demanded that he cease his work and leave the country. Members of the military or people linked to them are believed responsible for this threat. The family received further threats in February 1990.

Men imprisoned in Iran have often reported, after their release, that interrogators ·threatened their wives, mothers and sisters with torture or rape. One former detainee said that guards ordered him to speak with his sister by telephone. From her home telephone, she told her detained brother that government agents had come to her house and had threatened her with arrest unless he "confessed" to political activities.

A man arrested in Senegal during June 1984 testified after his release that guards had "parted my buttocks and poured in petrol. Then they called in my wife to show her the effect of the petrol in my anus." They struck his pregnant wife, the man continued. "Afterwards they took her to a classroom to rape her, and came and told me afterwards. They arrested my two children, aged two and three, and exposed them to the sun while refusing them their mother's help. They slapped my mother, who is very old." According to reports received from the Casamance region of southern Senegal, the practice of pouring petrol onto genitals and other sensitive parts of both men's and women's bodies continues at police and rural authorities' premises.

In April 1990 Salvadorian police raided the home of a woman and her husband, both of whom were church workers prominent in their parish, and detained their entire family. The police reportedly forced the wife's sister to strip during the raid and subjected her to sexual humiliation during long periods of interrogation. They also questioned the couple's four-year-old daughter at length about her father's work.

In a press interview, Gurmeet Kaur described the beatings she underwent while Indian police detained her in Punjab state in August 1989. The police were trying to find her husband, and she reported that she had lost contact with him five years earlier. In addition to assaulting her physically, she said, police threatened to kill her children.

Women who give birth in detention are vulnerable to threats and abuses related to their newborn infants. In Iraq, for example, detained women's babies have been taken from them. The women have been forced to listen to their infants' cries while being denied access to them and, therefore, the opportunity to comfort them.

Inadequate medical treatment and cruel or inhuman conditions of imprisonment

Women are often held under intolerable conditions in prisons and detention centres around the world and subjected to treatment which contravenes both domestic law and international norms. Governments which hold people under cruel, inhuman or degrading conditions are responsible for violating basic human rights. A lack of medical attention may place prisoners in a life-threatening situation, and surviving prisoners may face permanent injury as a result of inadequate medical care.

A Moroccan prisoner wrote from her cell in May 1987 that many women prisoners were suffering from several diseases "which are a result of torture and may be typical for prisoners". She explained,

"The prison authorities don't do anything to help us. We haven't even seen any medical specialists except for the physician of the prison.... His examination consisted of the simple question, 'Where does it hurt?' If you do get a prescription, you face another problem: getting the medication."

Pamela Majodina, who was arrested in September 1988 for possession of banned literature, alleged that South African police administered electric shocks to her genitals and assaulted her. At the beginning of 1989, she was suffering from urinary and gynaecological ailments. She said that the district surgeon who examined her at the Johannesburg Prison refused to record her complaint of torture and told her that she had simply developed an infection. The authorities released her in April 1989.

May al-Hafez was a post-graduate student of engineering when Syrian police arrested her in late 1987. She is a Palestinian who was born in Syria. Palestinians, especially alleged political activists, have been targets for many years of human rights abuses by Syrian authorities. Reports which emerged in February 1988 indicated that she had been tortured and that the authorities had subsequently denied her adequate medical treatment for leukaemia. Her physical condition was reportedly critical. She apparently remained in prison in late 1990 and may be a prisoner of conscience.

A Palestinian woman arrested by the Israeli authorities in 1988 was reportedly detained for several months, despite medical reports indicating that detention was not advisable. Terry Boullata, held on charges of membership of an illegal organization, was diagnosed as suffering from chronic active hepatitis. The authorities released her only after the condition worsened considerably.

A 26-year-old Iranian woman detained in Tehran's Evin Prison in September 1981 reported, "There must have been around 180 of us in the cell. There were hardly any sanitary facilities to speak of, and we had no change of underclothes and only one bar of soap for each group of six people to use for washing ourselves and our clothes. We found that after a while in detention, we stopped menstruating."

Pakistani authorities reportedly held more than a dozen women prisoners at the Lahore Fort military detention centre during 1982 and 1983. The women were held for periods of between several weeks and a year in filthy cells with inadequate toilet facilities. The cells contained no bedding, so the women slept on the floors. Some of the women were denied access to their families or defence counsel, and some were held in solitary confinement.

Conditions at Lexington Federal Prison in the United States of America have also been criticized by both human rights groups and the US authorities. Women prisoners held in the High Security Unit of the prison, according to a US Federal Court, were subjected to conditions which "skirted elemental standards of human decency". Amnesty International concluded that prolonged isolation in the unit, humiliating strip-searching, and restrictions detrimental to the prisoners' physical and mental health were oppressive conditions deliberately imposed by the authorities. Officials finally transferred the women to other facilities and closed the unit in 1988.

Soviet women held until 1987 in the "small zone" of the Mordovian Corrective Labour Colony suffered a range of harsh conditions. They were given food with inadequate nutritional value, and provided with only rudimentary medical facilities. Many of the women were confined periodically to a special punishment cell falling below international standards for humane treatment. The worst feature of the punishment cell, according to political prisoners held in the "small zone", was intense cold recorded as low as 8 degrees Centigrade. The women reportedly suffered a range of health problems, such as heart diseases and cystitis, because of their living conditions in the "small zone".

Indirect suffering caused by human rights abuses

"We sit in our homes day after day wondering what is happening to our children who are in prison", June Mlangeni stated at a press conference in December 1987. Representing the Federation of Transvaal Women in South Africa, she continued, "The effect of this type of worry causes the worst heartbreak any person can endure."

Knowledge that an arrest has been arbitrary and that imprisonment is unjust may add to the suffering of a detainee's family. If a prisoner is held under the constant threat of torture or ill-treatment, the lives of his or her relatives can be dominated by anguish. Other family members left at home may depend on a woman to provide support and advice at a time when the woman herself most needs such assistance. Some women may have to assume a new role: breadwinner for the family.

For detained women, absence from their families and fear for the fate of family members can also be a source of severe emotional distress. If the woman was the family breadwinner or the only parent living with young children, her detention may lead to dissolution of the family.

Six Senegalese women interviewed in 1985 said that they had been imprisoned for over a year and a half. They had been held incommunicado and had no news of their families; they knew nothing of the fates of their husbands and children.

The wife of a Guatemalan trade unionist knows nothing of her husband's fate, nine years after his "disappearance". He was among the many trade unionists who "disappeared" in 1981. "I cannot forget my husband, or the kind of man he was", she told Amnesty International. "He worked for a collective agreement at his plant, he marched more than 300 kilometres with the miners. He was arrested and beaten up, but he carried on with his trade union activities." She also faced severe economic difficulties because, as her husband was not legally dead, no state or other benefit was available to her. She feared that if she tried to find out what had happened to him she would risk being killed herself. "I had three children and a job, so I decided to dedicate myself to my work."

Jihad 'Abs was one of several people arrested in Tripoli, Lebanon, by Syrian forces in December 1986, on suspicion of membership of the Islamic Unification Movement. His wife was then pregnant with the couple's third child. The woman was widowed several days after the arrest, according to reports, when Jihad 'Abs died under torture.

Dr Manorani Saravanamuttu was at home in Colombo, Sri Lanka, with her son, Richard de Zoysa, when six armed men, one or two of whom were wearing police uniforms, stormed into their house on 18 February 1990. Richard de Zoysa was a well-known journalist, actor and poet. When Dr Saravanamuttu asked to see the men's identity cards, they threatened to kill her. They dragged her son from his bed and took him away with them. His naked body was found the next day with two gunshot wounds in the neck. She received an anonymous death threat in May 1990, apparently intended to deter her from pressing for a full inquiry into his death. "Mourn your son", the note said. "... Any other steps will result in your death".

Imprisonment on grounds of conscience
Women around the world have been imprisoned on grounds of conscience: because of their non-violent beliefs or activities, their ethnic origins, sex, religion or language.

Namat Issa was a senior civil servant at the Ethiopian Ministry of Foreign Affairs when she was detained. She was one of several hundred people of Oromo ethnic origin arrested in February 1980. Pregnant at the time of detention, she was reportedly tortured with severe beatings, primarily on the soles of her feet. The authorities apparently suspected her of having ties with opposition insurgents, although she was neither formally charged nor brought to trial. Amnesty International believed her to be a prisoner of conscience. In prison she gave birth to a son. The child, who had serious medical problems, remained with her in the Addis Ababa Central Prison until both were set free in an amnesty declared by the government in September 1989.

Tensions in Yugoslavia's Macedonia Republic, where some 20 per cent of the population are ethnic Albanians, continue. Peaceful demonstrators protested in October 1988 against educational policies in the republic that resulted in the elimination of many classes taught in the Albanian language.

Two young women were among the demonstrators arrested. Nafije Zendeli, aged 18, and Valdeta Fejzullai, aged 17, received prison sentences of four years after conviction on charges of "association for the purpose of hostile activity" and "counter-revolutionary undermining of the social order". They were imprisoned solely for the peaceful exercise of their rights to free expression and free association. The authorities reportedly released them in 1990 after international protest.

In Peru Carmela Ferro Estrada's husband "disappeared" after government soldiers took him and nine others for questioning. Two months later, in September 1988, Carmela Ferro Estrada travelled to the departmental capital to press for official acknowledgement of her husband's detention. She was arrested while queuing to receive food from the Peruvian Red Cross, charged with "terrorism" and imprisoned in the Abancay penitentiary. However, she is believed to be a prisoner of conscience, imprisoned simply because she sought information about her "disappeared" husband.

Inadequate or unfair legal proceedings

International agreements specify minimum standards for fair legal proceedings. All people taken into custody are entitled to basic legal rights. Article 10 of the Universal Declaration of Human Rights contains the provision that "everyone is entitled in full equality to a fair and public hearing by an independent and impartial tribunal". The International

Members of the Committee of Mothers of the "Disappeared", Political Prisoners, and Victims of Political Assassination in El Salvador (above) wait to present a petition to President Cristiani in October 1989. Appukutti Dewage Swarnalatha (right) "disappeared" in December 1988, one of many thousands of people who "disappeared" after being detained by the authorities in Sri Lanka during the 1980s. Peasant family (far right) in Peru's Ayacucho zone. The child on the woman's knee was conceived, she says, when she was raped by soldiers.

Covenant on Civil and Political Rights provides detailed guarantees of fair trial.

According to the Covenant, anyone who is charged with a criminal offence is entitled to be presumed innocent, to be promptly informed of the charges against them, to have adequate time and facilities for preparation of a defence, to communicate with counsel of their own choosing, and to be tried without undue delay by a competent, independent and impartial tribunal. Statements made as a result of torture or other cruel, inhuman or degrading treatment or other forms of coercion may not be introduced as evidence (except against a person accused of committing torture, ill-treatment or coercion). Every convicted person has the right of appeal to a higher tribunal. Nevertheless, women in every region of the world have been denied their rights to fair legal proceedings.

Countless prisoners of conscience have been jailed in Iran and thousands of people have been executed during the last decade following summary proceedings by Islamic Revolutionary Courts. Women prisoners of conscience convicted by Islamic Revolutionary Courts include Mariam Firouz, Malakeh Mohammadi and Zohreh Ghaeni. The three women were prominent members of the Tudeh Party, a political organization which was legal at the time of their arrest in 1983. Their support of the Tudeh Party seems to be the reason for their arrest. The women were not brought to trial until 1986. They had no legal representation during the proceedings and no right of appeal after conviction. The trials seemed to consist of little more than their appearance before a religious judge, followed by sentencing.

Mariam Firouz and Malakeh Mohammadi received death sentences, later commuted to prison terms of apparently indefinite duration. Zohreh Ghaeni received an eight-year prison sentence, which was designated to begin on the date of sentencing, although by then she had already spent three and a half years in custody. She was never informed of the precise charges against her.

Under laws passed in Sudan in 1989, the military governing body may determine procedures to be used by special courts both before and during trials. Defendants tried by these courts are not permitted proper legal representation, and the right to appeal is limited. Samira Hassan Mahdi, who worked in the judiciary department, was brought before a special court in December 1989 on charges of distributing anti-government leaflets. Her lawyer was not allowed to present evidence in her defence, refute

the charges against her, or cross-examine witnesses called by prosecutors in the special court that tried her. In fact, the lawyer was not permitted to speak in court. The special court convicted Samira Hassan Mahdi in December 1989 and sentenced her to three years' imprisonment. She is a prisoner of conscience, held in Omdurman prison near Khartoum.

Carole Richardson spent 15 years in a British prison before the authorities released her in 1989. She was arrested when she was 17 years old, and a court sentenced her in 1975 to life imprisonment for complicity in two bombing attacks. The judge at her trial stated that he would have sentenced her to death if United Kingdom law provided for such a punishment. The Court of Appeal ruled in 1989 that Carole Richardson and three co-defendants, known as the "Guildford Four", had been wrongly convicted because of police malpractice, including lying to the court about the uncorroborated "confessions" which had served as the basis for prosecution.

Proceedings in the trial in South Africa of Theresa Ramashamola and five other people evoked international protest. The authorities charged the "Sharpeville Six" with murder because they were allegedly among a crowd held responsible for the death of a Sharpeville township councillor. The killing occurred during civil unrest in 1984. At the conclusion of the "Sharpeville Six" trial in 1985, the court conceded that it had no proof of the defendants' direct involvement in the killing. Nevertheless, the court convicted them of murder and sentenced them to death. Amid widespread allegations that false or inadmissible evidence had been introduced at the trial, the South African authorities commuted the death sentences in 1988 to terms of imprisonment.

Charges against the "Manifesto" trial defendants in Mauritania included distribution of publications harmful to the national interest and propaganda "of a racial or ethnic character". The laws under which they were tried in 1986, and which remained in force in 1990, permit prosecution for peaceful political activities. The defendants appear to have been convicted on the basis of statements they made to police during pre-trial detention. A 22-year-old woman among the defendants told the court that her treatment in pre-trial detention included rape by a police commissioner. The authorities failed to investigate her allegations of torture, and maintained that officials later claimed that such an offence was "impossible" in their country. The woman had no access to a lawyer until the trial began. The court sentenced her to six months' imprisonment.

Seviye Köprü was also convicted on the basis of a "confession" made to police. She testified before a Turkish state security court that, during pre-trial detention in 1987, police laid her on the floor, held her arms, and kicked her. They forced her legs apart, and one of them raped her. "While the man was raping me, someone slapped my face. After that, I don't remember anything", she said. The court did not investigate the rape allegation and convicted her in 1988 of membership of an illegal organization.

The Israeli authorities have reportedly held some 12,000 people in administrative detention, without charge or trial, since the beginning of the Palestinian uprising in December 1987. Administrative detention orders often cover a period of six months, although they can be issued for a period of one year. Husniyya 'Abd al-Qader, who lives in the Balata refugee camp in the West Bank and organizes kintergartens and sewing workshops, received her second administrative detention order in October 1989. A judge rejected her appeal against the order the following month, alleging that Husniyya 'Abd al-Qader was a prominent opposition activist. She was released in April 1990, when the administrative detention order expired.

Amnesty International's information indicates that Husniyya 'Abd al-Qader may have been a prisoner of conscience, detained solely for her non-violent political beliefs and activities. As in the case of virtually every Palestinian placed in administrative detention by the Israeli authorities during recent years, she was not given details of the accusation against her and therefore denied an adequate opportunity to exercise effectively her right to challenge the detention order.

Scores of alleged political opponents or critics of the government have been detained in recent years without charge or trial in the eastern provinces of Saudi Arabia. They have no legal means of challenging their detention and Amnesty International has received frequent reports that detainees have been tortured and ill-treated. Makkiyya 'Abdullah Hamdam was detained in July 1986, after she had attempted to discover the fate of her husband, who had been detained in May. She reportedly remained in detention until the end of 1986, although she was not charged with an offence.

The Somali authorities permitted Fahima Dahir Jama, a 25-year-old student, to attend only the initial part of her trial. She met her lawyer for the first time on the day the trial began in mid-1986, and the specific charges against her were not revealed. She had no opportunity to hear the case against her or to present evidence in her defence. The National Security Court convicted her in May 1986 of belonging to an insurgent group and sentenced her to life imprisonment. She was freed, however, in 1989.

Under the Sri Lankan Prevention of Terrorism Act (PTA), people may be arrested, denied information about the reason for arrest, and held "in such a place and subject to such conditions as may be determined" by government officials. Jancy Soundranayagan, an undergraduate university student, was detained under the PTA in March 1986. The authorities gave no reasons for her arrest and brought no charges against her throughout her detention. She was released in 1989.

A majority of the death sentences handed down in Nigeria follow trials before Robbery and Firearms Tribunals, special courts operating outside the ordinary judicial system and which do not conform to international standards for a fair trial. Convicted defendants have no right of appeal to a higher court. In addition, inefficiency and corruption reportedly mar many police investigations prior to trial before these courts. Poor and otherwise disadvantaged Nigerians appear to be frequent targets of arrests for offences tried before the special tribunals.

A number of Nigerian women have been sentenced to death after conviction. However, it is not clear whether the authorities commuted their sentences or hanged them out of public view. A tribunal sentenced Clara Baada to be hanged, according to reports received in January 1988, following conviction on charges of armed robbery. Although four male co-defendants were executed in public by firing squad, Clara Baada apparently was not hanged because of a defective gallows in Plateau state. Information about her subsequent fate has not been available.

Cruel and degrading punishments
The Universal Declaration of Human Rights, the International Covenant on Civil and Political Rights, the UN Convention against Torture and Other Cruel, Inhuman or Degrading Treatment or Punishment, and other international legal instruments prohibit cruel, inhuman, or degrading punishments. Amnesty International considers every execution to be a human rights violation, because the death penalty is the extreme form of cruel, inhuman and degrading punishment. The death penalty also denies victims the fundamental

right to life proclaimed in the Universal Declaration of Human Rights.

Women have been executed in numerous countries during recent years. The US has the largest death row population in the world, numbering over 2,300 people by late 1990. In the US, 30 women remained on death row in October 1990. The authorities in North Carolina executed Velma Barfield by lethal injection in November 1984. An Illinois court tried Paula Cooper for a murder committed when she was 15 years old and sentenced her to death in July 1986. However, in July 1989 her sentence was commuted to 60 years' imprisonment.

The Islamic Penal Code of Iran provides for death by stoning as punishment for adulterers and certain other offenders. The Penal Code stipulates that "in the punishment of stoning to death, the stones should not be so large that the person dies on being hit by one or two of them, nor should they be so small that they could not be defined as stones". At least 24 of the more than 40 people reportedly stoned to death in Iran during 1989 were women, executed for offences such as adultery and prostitution.

Many Pakistani women face the threat of cruel punishments under the Hudood Ordinances promulgated in 1979. The offence of *zina* — wilful extramarital sexual intercourse — can be punished with public lashing and stoning to death. Although men and women have been sentenced to stoning to death no such sentence had been carried out by the end of 1990.

Women who have been raped risk charges of *zina*, whether or not they report the assault. If a woman becomes pregnant as the result of an unreported rape, she may be charged with *zina*. If a woman reports rape, she bears the onus of proof. A number of Pakistani women have accused men of rape and failed to prove their cases in court. The male defendants have been acquitted, while the women plaintiffs have been charged with *zina*.

Pakistani police officers reportedly raped two women held on charges of *zina* at a Lahore police station during 1988. After an official inquiry into the case, the Lahore High Court found that the women had been raped and otherwise tortured and that the charges against them were false. The authorities failed to arrest the officers allegedly involved in the rapes, however, and the *zina* charges case against the women had not been withdrawn by March 1990.

Pakistani authorities prosecuted a blind woman for *zina* in 1983. She had accused her landlord and his son of raping her. At their trial, Safia Bibi had been unable to identify her attackers because of her sight loss. The court acquitted the two men, then convicted her of *zina* and sentenced her to be flogged publicly and imprisoned. Local and international protests followed these proceedings, and judicial officials acquitted Safia Bibi on appeal.

Another Pakistani woman was sentenced, with her second husband, in 1989 to death by stoning. Her first husband claimed that she had remarried without legal divorce, and a court convicted both her and her second husband of adultery. Four other men were also sentenced to death by stoning as accomplices to the second marriage. Their executions were stayed, however, and the case apparently had not yet been heard by an appeal court by mid-1990.

Under international law, corporal punishment such as flogging constitutes cruel, inhuman or degrading punishment. Public floggings have been reported in several countries, including Sudan. Human rights monitors have indicated that street vendors operating without a licence, most of them women, have been summarily tried in market places since the 1989 coup in Sudan. Hastily constituted Public Order Emergency Courts have convicted vendors and ordered them to be punished on the spot by flogging.

In Iran flogging is a punishment for offences such as failure to observe veiling or other clothing regulations. The authorities reportedly impose this punishment inconsistently; in some cases women are reported to have been flogged on the open streets without any legal proceedings whatsoever.

The International Covenant on Civil and Political Rights prohibits the execution of pregnant women, and no pregnant woman is known to have been judicially executed in the past decade.

A legal journal article published in China during 1986, however, suggested that "some judicial departments" were unclear about whether abortions could be imposed to render pregnant women eligible for the death penalty. The authors of "A General Account of Criminal Law Research in New China" stated that forcing a pregnant woman to terminate the pregnancy before prosecution would contravene China's Criminal Law. According to the article, some judicial officials held the opinion that abortion before or at the time of trial would render a woman eligible for the death penalty. The legal issues raised included the role of China's national birth control policy in official decisions to mandate the termination of a pregnancy.

'Disappearance' and extrajudicial execution

Government authorities and individuals acting under official orders or with official acquiescence have killed women wholly outside the framework of the law. Some women have been arrested or abducted, then never seen again. Victims of "disappearance" around the world, like the victims of extrajudicial killing, include men, women, and children from many sectors of society.

Victims of "disappearance" do not, of course, simply vanish; one or more government agents know what has happened to them. If the body is never found, the family of a "disappeared" person lives with conflicting hopes and fears, never fully able to give up the search, mourn, or begin the process of healing after such an experience of loss. The UN General Assembly has stressed that families of the "disappeared" have a right to know the fate of their relatives.

Ana María del Carmen Pérez was in the later stages of pregnancy when she "disappeared" in 1976, one of the thousands who met such a fate during the "dirty war" waged by Argentine military authorities against opposition in the country. Forensic scientists finally identified her body in 1989 among exhumed remains. Her unborn child had been killed by two shots fired into her abdomen. A presidential pardon granted in 1989 prevents prosecution of Argentine military officers responsible for such atrocities.

Some 200 children reportedly "disappeared" with their parents or were born to women held in secret Argentine detention centres between 1976 and 1983. Infants were taken from their imprisoned mothers at birth. Although the fate of numerous mothers remains unknown, evidence has increasingly emerged that many of the infants were given illegally to childless couples associated with the military. The Grandmothers of the Plaza de Mayo, a group of Argentine human rights activists, have been assisted by genetic scientists in tracing the whereabouts of their "disappeared" grandchildren. Fifty of the "disappeared" children had been located by late 1990.

Hundreds of Salvadorians have "disappeared" during the past decade, and government authorities have taken few steps to investigate the victims' fate. Several people witnessed the arrest of Sara Cristina Chan-Chan Medina, a photo-journalist working for a major trade union federation, in August 1989. Uniformed members of the Salvadorian Air Force arrested her in the street. An Air Force official told the young woman's mother several days later that her daughter had been arrested by the Air Force and then transferred to Treasury Police custody. The Air Force and Treasury Police, however, continue to deny that they ever held her in custody. Sara Cristina Chan-Chan Medina and Juan Francisco Massi Chávez, who was arrested with her, are still missing.

Many women are among the hundreds of people who have "disappeared" in the Western Sahara since Morocco's annexation of the region in 1975. A wave of arrests preceded the visit of Moroccan King Hassan II to Laayoune in March 1985. Police arrested at least five women two days before the King's arrival, and all of them subsequently "disappeared". Sebbaha ment Mohamed ould Lehbib, pregnant at the time of her arrest, was one of the Laayoune victims. Another was 40-year-old Salka ment Najem ould Omar Lahsen. Police knocked down the door of her house, according to reports, and arrested her on suspicion of distributing opposition leaflets.

In the Philippines dozens of activists involved in lawful non-governmental organizations "disappeared" in 1989. During the first half of 1990, at least 40 more activists "disappeared". Members of the military and some government officials have labelled the organizations as fronts for illegal opposition groups. Two victims of "disappearance" in the Philippines worked for the Ecumenical Center for Research and Development, a research group which services local grassroots organizations. Maria Nonna Santa Clara and Angelina Llenaresas were last seen in the custody of military personnel in April 1989. The military authorities later denied holding them in detention, and witnesses who testified at the *habeas corpus* proceedings on their behalf reportedly have received death threats.

Twenty-two-year-old Amelia Tena "disappeared" in May 1990 after armed men believed to be members of the Philippines Intelligence Service abducted her. A witness to the abduction was able to identify by name two of the assailants but, fearing retaliation by the military, has gone into hiding. Amelia Tena is a member of Youth for Democracy and Nationalism, an opposition group targeted by the military in 1988. Several members of the group were reportedly tortured in custody and then "disappeared" during 1988.

Men dressed in civilian clothing bundled Amparo Tordecilla Trujillo into a taxi in Bogota, Colombia, on 25 April 1989. The 28-year-old mother of two young children has not been seen since then. A Public Ministry investigation into her "disappearance" reportedly found that the taxi was registered

Amparo Tordecilla Trujillo (above) was abducted in Bogota, Colombia, in April 1989. The 28-year-old mother of two young children, she has not been seen since then. In the Philippines, Maria Nonna Santa Clara (right) also "disappeared" in April 1989. She was last seen in the custody of military personnel. She worked for a research group servicing local grassroots organizations.

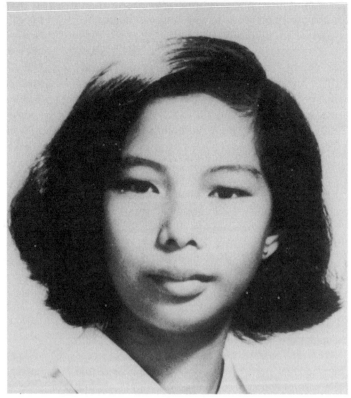

Mothers of the "disappeared" in Argentina (top) stage a demonstration in August 1983 against legislation intended to stop investigation of human rights violations. Families of political prisoners in Morocco (above left) demonstrate for their relatives' release. Guatemalan Indian women (above right) searching for "disappeared" relatives.

as an official military intelligence vehicle. Military intelligence authorities initially told investigators that Amparo Tordecilla Trujillo had been arrested. Ministry of Defence officials, however, later denied her detention. These officials reportedly said that the woman observed in the taxi was, in fact, a military agent.

Of the many thousands of people who have "disappeared" in Sri Lanka during the 1980s, only a small proportion are women. Two of the "disappeared" women were arrested by soldiers in December 1988. Press reports cited statements by detainees released from the Kotigala army camp about two women, Appukutti Dewage Swarnalatha, also known as "Deepika", and Chamani Muthuhetti. The former detainees said that the two women had been raped by camp guards. They also reported that camp guards had dragged the women, believed to be in their twenties, to the rear of the compound. Then gunshots were heard from that direction, followed by the odour of burning bodies. The authorities have not acknowledged the two women's detention, and *habeas corpus* petitions have been filed on their behalf.

Many victims of extrajudicial execution and "disappearance" by Sri Lankan security forces or paramilitary groups have been young people whom the authorities suspected of being involved in the activities of an armed opposition group. Other victims have been reportedly killed simply because they were residents of communities considered sympathetic to that group.

Thousands of civilians have been extrajudicially executed by government troops during the Peruvian military's operations against violent opposition forces. The forces of the clandestine Communist Party of Peru "Shining Path" have continued to murder captured security forces personnel. "Shining Path" has also been responsible for the execution-style killing of civilians, sometimes after torture and mock trials.

Women, as well as men and children, were victims of apparent extrajudicial execution by government troops in the Huanta province of Ayacucho Department during August 1990. Surviving members of the Iquichi peasant community near Uchuraccay reported that three days after a confrontation between government forces and an armed opposition group, soldiers and members of a local civil defence organization detained and shot dead 16 villagers. According to reports, members of the Iquichi peasant community had refused to join forces against the

insurgents because they believed that soldiers wanted to protect themselves by using villagers as "shields".

Nonyamezelo Victoria Mxenge was a prominent South African human rights lawyer and leader of the Natal Organisation of Women. When she was shot and killed by four assailants in August 1985, she was defending 16 leading members of the United Democratic Front opposition organization who were facing treason charges. An inquest court conducting an inquiry into her death concluded in 1989 that her assailants could not be identified.

However, the suspicion remains that an officially sanctioned "death squad" was responsible for her death. In late 1989 the controversy over her death and that of other activists who have died in South Africa in unexplained circumstances came under national and international scrutiny following the death row confession of a former police officer. He claimed to have been involved in the 1981 murder of Griffiths Mxenge, Victoria Mxenge's husband, who was a prominent lawyer and activist. His claims and those of several other former police officers, regarding their activities as members of an alleged police "death squad", became the subject of a government-appointed commission of inquiry in 1990. The report of the commission, whose narrow terms of reference have been widely criticized, was released in November 1990. The judge presiding over the inquiry rejected the allegations that the police operated a "death squad". He reached no conclusions regarding responsibility for the murders of Victoria and Griffiths Mxenge.

In Turkey, no official inquiry into the death of Güllü Zeren has been reported. The 45-year-old Turkish woman, a member of the Kurdish ethnic minority, died of gunshot wounds in May 1988. According to an official version of the event, she had been ordered to halt as she passed by the Forests' Department building in Diyarbakir province. When she failed to respond to the order, she was shot.

Questions of extrajudicial killing have arisen in Güllü Zeren's case, as in numerous other killings during recent years in southeastern Turkey. One of Güllü Zeren's sons reportedly lodged a complaint at a local police station about the killing. Police allegedly held him there for two days and beat him in an attempt to intimidate others from inquiring into the shooting. Güllü Zeren was a widow with four children aged between eight and 16.

Hundreds of extrajudicial executions in India have been reported annually during the past decade. Irom

Ongbi Bino Devi is among the unarmed civilians who have been apparently shot dead in Manipur state. After unidentified gunmen ambushed a Central Reserve Police patrol in April 1980, security forces reportedly herded villagers from the area into a field. Irom Ongbi Bino Devi, who was pregnant, hid in her granary. Upon discovering her, members of the security forces shot and killed her. The Manipur authorities later granted financial compensation to her family.

Twelve members of a Colombian judicial commission investigating abuses attributed to military and paramilitary forces were shot dead during January 1989 in a remote rural area of the central Magdalena Medio region. Mariela Morales Caro, an examining magistrate, was among the victims of apparent extrajudicial execution. She belonged to the Colombian Judicial Workers' Association, a group which estimates that more than 300 judicial employees and more than 50 judges have been killed since 1980. Many of the killings have occurred in the context of drugs-related cases. Evidence in other cases, however, suggests that judicial officials were threatened and killed because of their investigations into human rights violations.

Two Colombian army officers and six civilian members of a paramilitary group were convicted in June 1990 of murdering Mariela Morales Caro and her 11 co-workers. The defendants received prison sentences of between eight and 30 years. Although the civilians were in custody in late 1990, the army lieutenant had "escaped" from the military base where he was being held and the whereabouts of the other officer are not known.

Basic rights are interdependent; the denial of one right may destroy a person's ability to exercise other rights. When a woman is raped in detention by law enforcement officials to force a "confession" from her, the introduction of that "confession" during legal proceedings compounds torture with an unfair trial. By detaining women for the peaceful exercise of their rights to free association and free expression, government authorities have prevented them from organizing for the protection of other basic human rights.

Human rights abuses cannot be rated on a scale of severity. If government authorities permit one type of violation, numerous other violations may follow. Every violation warrants public protest.

4

Women in peril

The preceding descriptions of human rights violations against women show that none of the world's major systems of government is exempt from criticism. Grave human rights abuses have been committed by governments with widely differing ideologies in Africa, the Americas, Asia and the Pacific, Europe, and the Middle East.

Patterns of gross violations are often evident in situations of social or political turmoil. Much of the torture, killing, and inhuman conditions of imprisonment described earlier in this report takes place in the context of such turmoil.

Civil, ethnic, and nationalist struggles can unleash waves of government repression when the authorities ignore human rights safeguards. No situation or circumstance, however, can justify denial of fundamental human rights. All governments are responsible for ensuring human rights protection at all times.

In situations of armed conflict, non-combatant women and their families can be caught in repressive government operations. Women activists pressing for rights protection amid situations of unrest have been targeted for abuses, including arbitrary arrest, torture, and extrajudicial killing. Women refugees are also among the people especially vulnerable to human rights violations committed by government authorities.

Situations of civil unrest, disturbance, and conflict

Civil unrest may range from local disputes to nation-wide conflicts between a government and one or more sectors of society. Complex cultural, political, and economic issues may be involved. The tensions find expression through numerous peaceful, as well as violent, channels. Many governments have failed to maintain international human rights norms in areas of civil unrest and conflict. Women in these areas have been victims of human rights violations because of their strengths, such as community leadership skills, or because of their vulnerabilities. The following examples of human rights violations committed in the context of unrest are by no means comprehensive.

China

The Chinese Government created an atmosphere of terror in June 1989, when troops attacked peaceful pro-democracy protesters in Beijing and other cities. At least 1,000 people were killed in the capital city. One of the last civilians to leave Tiananmen Square on the night of 3 June described the deaths of several young women in the Square. He said that he saw "one of the temporary tents erected by students with posts and covered by canvas. The tent was open towards the south. There were about seven girls inside. The armoured personnel carriers were moving down very slowly, but without stopping. I rushed to the tent and told the girls to leave, but they refused. I dragged one of them towards the west.... I rushed back to the tent. There were three other people trying to persuade the girls to leave. By that time, one of the armoured personnel carriers had come very close to the tent. I ran in front, shouting at them to stop.... The armoured personnel carrier continued to move ahead. The tent collapsed, trapping the girls inside. The armoured personnel carrier went straight over it."

An official Chinese television broadcast warned on 7 June, a few days after the killings in Beijing, that troops were authorized to dispose of anyone who resisted arrest. Numerous arbitrary arrests have been reported since mid-1989. Among the women arrested were: Cheng Mingxia, a leader of the unofficial Beijing student movement arrested in Beijing during July 1989; Ma Ziyi, a historian and lecturer arrested in Shanghai in early October 1989; and Dan Jing, a journalist working with the *New China News* when she was arrested in Changsha on 7 June 1989. All of the women were detained solely for the peaceful exercise of their basic rights. Reports indicate that Dan Jing was being forced to perform hard labour in late 1990. Ma Ziyi was reportedly released on bail and awaiting trial at that time.

The Chinese authorities also arrested Wang Zhihong, in November 1989 as she travelled to Canton along an escape route to Hong Kong. She was eight months pregnant at the time of arrest and gave birth prematurely in prison. Her child did not survive. She was released in mid-November 1990, after being held for a year without charge.

Mauritania

Intercommunal violence claimed hundreds of lives in Mauritania during April 1989. Subsequent security force operations against black Mauritanians have resulted in human rights violations reaching levels unprecedented in the country in recent years. In November 1989, for example, three members of the National Guard fired on a group of women and children outside their village of Nere-Walo in the Kaedi area of southern Mauritania. They killed a young woman and two children in the attack.

Government forces summarily expelled more than 50,000 black Mauritanians to Senegal during 1989, committing torture and extrajudicial executions in the process. Soldiers reportedly raped young women from the village of Toumbel in June 1989, then forced them to cross the river into Senegal naked. National Guardsmen and soldiers are believed to have committed most of the rapes reported by former detainees.

A 25-year-old black woman held for three months in a Nouakchott police station was transferred in February 1990 to the security police headquarters in Rosso, according to reports, then to a military post in the Ould Mogheina area. Soldiers at the post raped her for an entire night, she said, before expelling her from the country by throwing her into the Senegal River.

USSR

Ethnic violence reported in the USSR during 1990 has raised questions of the authorities' failure to intervene for the protection of citizens. For example, the official Soviet news agency TASS said that police and soldiers in Azerbaydzhan took no effective steps to protect Armenian citizens attacked by Azeris in January. At least 30 Armenians were killed, including two women reportedly thrown to their deaths from a high building and one pregnant woman allegedly burned alive.

Situations of armed conflict

Article 3 of each of the 1949 Geneva Conventions, which applies to cases of non-international armed conflict, prohibits acts against non-combatants such as "murder of all kinds", "violence to life", torture, the taking of hostages, and "outrages upon personal dignity, in particular humiliating and degrading treatment".

Protocol I to the 1949 Geneva Conventions, addressing international armed conflicts, contains in Article 76 provisions relating specifically to women. Women "shall be protected in particular against rape, forced prostitution, and any other form of indecent assault", the article states. Pregnant women and mothers with dependent infants, according to the Protocol, are entitled to special consideration in these situations of international conflict.

Neither civilian nor military authorities are exempt from the obligation to guarantee all citizens' basic rights. Breakdowns in military discipline which result in abuses can never be tolerated.

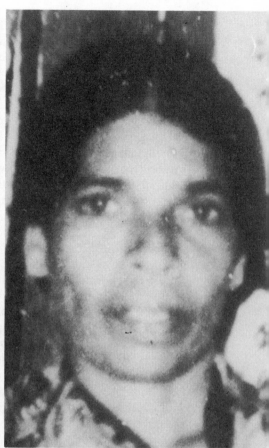

(Above) Demonstrator carries a photograph of Mairead Farrell in a 1980 Belfast protest in support of political prisoners in 1980. She was then one of four women on hunger-strike in Armagh prison, Northern Ireland. She was released from prison some eight years later. Shortly afterwards, she and two other unarmed IRA members were shot dead in Gibraltar by members of the British army. Thangaratman Sangaralingam (above right) "disappeared" with her daughters Kayathiri Vino, Kanagambikai and Chanthirika Sangaralingam (right) after being arrested in November 1987 by members of the Indian Peace Keeping Force stationed in Sri Lanka.

(Above) When violence erupts, women civilians are often caught in the crossfire. This woman was injured during intercommunal disturbances in northeast Burundi, August 1988.

Women in Kuwait City (left) protest against the Iraqi invasion of Kuwait in August 1990. Reports of arbitrary arrest, torture, rape and killing followed the invasion. A 25-year-old woman was shot and killed when troops opened fire on a group of women and young people protesting against the invasion.

Colombia

Violence against civilians has escalated in Colombia during the past two years. Armed opposition groups have confronted government authorities, in circumstances complicated by the widely publicized actions of drug-traffickers. Most victims of political violence, however, have been civilians.

More than 3,500 Colombians have been victims of extrajudicial execution since mid-1987. Army troops arrested 15-year-old Sandra Patricia Vélez near her home in Yondó, Antioquia department, in February 1989. Her fate remained unknown until September 1990, when her body was found in a shallow grave. Sandra Patricia Vélez was pregnant at the time of her arrest.

Many of the extrajudicial killings in Colombia have been carried out by paramilitary "death squads" linked to army officers. Members of the judiciary attempting to investigate human rights abuses involving government agents became targets of death threats and killings in 1989. Judge María Elena Díaz Pérez was one of these victims, killed by unidentified gunmen in July 1989.

At least three other women were among the judges who have received death threats. These warnings are often followed by murder in Colombia. The Colombian Government has failed to curb "death squad" activity.

Iraq

Shortly after the August 1990 invasion of Kuwait by Iraqi forces, reports of the arbitrary arrest, torture and killing of civilians began to emerge from Kuwait. Iraqi soldiers reportedly fired on a group of some 35 women and young people peacefully demonstrating against the invasion in Kuwait City. An eyewitness to this incident said that troops shot a 25-year-old woman in the head. She died in hospital. Scores of hangings on the Kuwait University grounds also have been reported.

Released detainees have described routine torture by Iraqi military and intelligence agents operating in Kuwait. The methods of torture described include electric shocks, prolonged beatings, and threats of sexual assault and execution. Numerous rapes committed by Iraqi soldiers have also been reported. During the week following the invasion, soldiers reportedly raped three Filipino women and a British woman held in their custody. Later reports contain allegations of soldiers raping Kuwaiti and other Arab women.

Hundreds of Kuwaitis and other nationals were believed to be held during September 1990 and later in the year in detention centres or prisons in Iraq and Kuwait. The Iraqi authorities apparently detained women, as well as men and children, for offences such as possession of opposition literature or the Kuwaiti flag. Reports indicate that such offences were punishable by execution.

Israel and the Occupied Territories

Widespread human rights violations have been committed during the Palestinian uprising, or *intifada*, in the Israeli Occupied Territories which began in December 1987. The abuses include unjustifiable killings and punitive beatings. Some 12,000 Palestinians have been administratively detained, without charge, trial, or provision of adequate information about the reasons for detention. Administrative detention orders can be issued for periods of up to 12 months and can be renewed indefinitely.

Thousands of Palestinians have been interrogated, often accompanied by torture or ill-treatment, and tried by military courts. Palestinian women have reported in recent years that interrogators threatened them with rape and subjected them to sexually humiliating practices.

While repeatedly stating their intention to respect the "humanitarian provisions" of the Fourth Geneva Convention, relative to the protection of civilians, the Israeli Government has refused to acknowledge that the Convention constitutes binding international law regarding Israel's actions in the Occupied Territories.

Mozambique

Although the Mozambique Government has taken significant steps in recent years to protect human rights, violations by government agents have been reported. For example, some women have alleged that they were tortured by police after their arrest. Several women were apparently accused of witchcraft and summarily executed in October 1987 by militia who were acting illegally.

The torture and killing of prisoners by political organizations other than governments has been a human rights concern in Mozambique throughout the 1980s in the context of continuing fighting between government troops and the Mozambique National Resistance, known as RENAMO or RNM. Opposition groups do not have the status of governments in terms of international human rights law. Amnesty International has monitored abuses committed by groups such as RENAMO, however, when they possess certain essential attributes of governments. These attributes include exercise of effective power over substantial territory and population.

RENAMO insurgents have reportedly forced civilians to act as porters for them and have taken young girls and adult women into custody to meet combatants' sexual demands. Punishments for refusal to participate in sexual acts have included severe beatings or execution, according to reports. RENAMO combatants are reported to have frequently raped women.

When men have escaped from areas under strict RENAMO control, their wives and children allegedly have been executed in retribution. RENAMO combatants also have reportedly killed the wives and children of local officials during the 1980s.

Myanmar

Counter-insurgency campaigns in Myanmar, formerly Burma, have been accompanied throughout the 1980s and into 1990 by gross human rights violations against ethnic minority communities. Widespread torture and extrajudicial executions have been reported, and soldiers have abducted villagers at random to serve as porters. Thousands of members of the ethnic minorities in areas of counter-insurgency operations have fled their homes since the mid-1980s.

Rape is among the human rights violations often reported in Myanmar. While interrogating a farmer from Naw Kwa village in January 1987 about alleged opposition sympathies, soldiers raped his wife. Rape apparently has been used to punish villagers in Swi Ta Pi, where residents were suspected of supporting insurgents. Soldiers have also reportedly raped women, including an 11-year-old girl, as punishment for disobeying official regulations.

Myanmar troops have taken the wives or other female relatives of suspected political opponents as hostages, according to reports, while soldiers searched for the suspects. A rice farmer from Ta U Khi village testified that soldiers arrested her in October 1986. An interrogator "put a gun barrel behind my right ear and said he would shoot me if I didn't tell them where my brother was", she said. A farmer from Kru Yi village, the 44-year-old mother of seven, testified that soldiers kicked her in the back, chest, and face, then detained her for eight months without charge or trial in an attempt to force her husband to surrender to them. Soldiers also tried to force a woman from Ya Pu village to engage in sexual acts before ordering her, she said, "to send a message to the village asking my husband to come the following day to the [army] camp".

Peru

The severe deterioration of human rights observance in Peru coincided with major government operations to combat violent opposition groups. All or part of 11 departments in the country and two-thirds of the population had been placed under state of emergency regulations by 1990. These regulations give the military broad powers of arrest and detention. Members of the political-military command in emergency zones have seized, tortured and murdered people suspected of supporting the opposition. Soldiers have also conducted reprisal raids against entire villages.

Peruvian women have been subjected to an escalating number of grave human rights abuses. Members of the security forces appear to act with impunity in committing rape and other forms of torture or ill-treatment, and in killing civilians in the course of counter-insurgency operations.

The victims include leaders of women's groups, teachers, and the wives of suspected government opponents. Troops raided the Santa Ana community in Ayacucho department in June 1989, according to reports. Three elderly men were killed, and young women reportedly were taken into a church and raped.

In June 1990 Guadalupe Ccallocunto reportedly "disappeared" in the city of Ayacucho. She was vice-president of the Association of Relatives of Detained and "Disappeared" People in the Emergency Zone and an active member of the Peace and Justice Service. Human rights monitors in both Ayacucho and Lima believe that members of the army detained her. The military had repeatedly harassed her in the months preceding her "disappearance", and she remained among the "disappeared" in late 1990.

Philippines

Despite repeated assurances by the Philippines Government of its commitment to protecting human rights, serious patterns of abuses have been reported throughout 1989 and 1990. Hundreds of alleged opponents or critics of the government have been extrajudicially executed during this period, and government or government-backed forces have killed civilians in areas of suspected insurgent activity.

When Philippines Constabulary soldiers opened fire in May 1990 on the home of Crisanto Losande in May 1990, they killed his 23-year-old wife, Edna, and their two children. Crisanto Losande was apparently thought to sympathize with or participate in opposition activities. The children were aged eight months and two years. Reports indicate that the military intensified operations in eastern Rizal province, where the Losande home is located, during the first half of 1990. Community leaders there claim that the military considers some lawful farmers' associations and environmental groups in the region to be fronts for armed opposition.

Paramilitary groups, evidently established or supported by the military, are responsible for numerous abductions and killings in the Philippines. In May 1987 a paramilitary group reportedly took into custody two women belonging to the Alliance of Poor Farmers. The bodies of Marilyn Negro and Teresita Udtohan were found in July. Both had been mutilated. Teresita Udtohan, who was about six months pregnant when arrested, had been slashed in the abdomen.

Josepha Padcayan, a community health worker, remained in secret military detention in late 1990. Army troops arrested her in November 1989 during intensive military operations against insurgents. She reportedly was delivering relief goods to villages affected by the fighting at the time of her arrest.

Somalia

Somali insurgents and government troops have engaged in heavy fighting since 1988. In 1988 government military personnel extrajudicially executed large numbers of unarmed civilians in the north belonging to the Issaq clan, including women and children. The government associated membership of this clan with membership of armed opposition forces. The authorities have also arrested hundreds of Issaqs living in different regions and detained them without trial. Hundreds of thousands fled to Ethiopia or were displaced inside Somalia.

Mothers and their children attempting to flee from the fighting in northwest Somalia were detained and killed by the military. In addition, the military has killed villagers in reprisal for suspected support of opposition forces. Hawa Abdillahi was among the victims of extrajudicial execution, a civilian woman shot by soldiers in late 1988 during operations against villages in the north.

Women and their children have also been victims of extrajudicial executions in other parts of the country as fighting between new rebel forces and government troops intensified in 1989 and 1990.

(Above) Thousands of Iraqi Kurds sought refuge in Turkey in August and September 1988 after chemical weapon attacks against Kurdish villages in northern Iraq.
(Right) Women who have sought refuge from armed conflict, in Clappenburg camp, Trincomalee, northeastern Sri Lanka.
(Opposite) This Issaq woman lost her right foot when she trod on a Somali army landmine during her flight from fighting between government troops and insurgents in northern Somalia in 1988. Large numbers of unarmed civilians belonging to the Issaq clan were extrajudicially executed by government soldiers.

The Goddess of Democracy, a statue erected by Chinese students who occupied Tiananmen Square in May and June 1989. When the square was cleared by the Chinese army, several young women were crushed to death by military vehicles.

United Kingdom

Amnesty International has criticized several policies and practices apparently initiated by the United Kingdom Government in response to violent attacks by opposition groups from Northern Ireland. During 1989 the United Kingdom authorities began an inquiry into judicial policy issues, following the release of the "Guildford Four" when the Appeal Court found that they had been wrongly convicted because of police malpractice. The issues being addressed by the inquiry include the use of uncorroborated confessions as the basis for prosecution, the adequacy of safeguards for suspects in alleged terrorist cases, and the procedures used to investigate possible miscarriages of justice.

Disputed killings by security forces in Northern Ireland since 1982 have raised serious questions about the procedures used by the United Kingdom Government to investigate such events and about legislation governing the use of lethal force by the security forces. The cases of Mairead Farrell and two other members of the Irish Republican Army, both of them men, who were shot dead by Special Air Services forces in Gibraltar during March 1988, also raised questions about government policies and inquest procedures. The three were unarmed when they were killed. Amnesty International considers that government inquest procedures left unanswered the question of whether their deaths resulted from an official policy of deliberate planned killings targeting suspected members of armed opposition groups.

Points of entry, refugee camps and other centres

A majority of adults who flee their countries are women, according to the Office of the UN High Commissioner for Refugees. In an article published in 1988, a legal adviser to the UN High Commissioner described his findings about the special vulnerabilities of women refugees to several forms of abuse. When fleeing persecution, some women become separated from their families and lose the protections provided by a community or familiar cultural milieu. "Rape, abduction, sexual harassment, physical violence and the not infrequent obligation to grant 'sexual favours' in return for documentation and/or relief goods remain a distressing reality for many women refugees", the legal adviser stated.

The situation of South East Asian refugees fleeing their countries by boat received international attention during the 1980s. According to the legal adviser, "Hundreds of women were raped, abducted and killed by pirates". While acknowledging the difficulty in confirming information about abuses committed in border areas, refugee camps and other locations, he said that "the various forms and circumstances in which women refugees suffer violence and sexual abuse are nevertheless fairly well documented." He said that women may be at risk of abuse by the authorities who regulate entry to a country, detention facilities and resettlement procedures.

In addition, refugees may face a grave threat in their flight from persecution in the form of *refoulement*, or forcible return to a country where their life or freedom is at risk because of their race, religion, nationality, membership of a particular social group or political opinion. The Universal Declaration of Human Rights proclaims that "everyone has the right to seek and enjoy in other countries asylum from persecution". The 1951 UN Convention relating to the Status of Refugees prohibits *refoulement*. Yet some governments subject asylum-seekers to biased or obstructive practices, and in many cases people have been forcibly returned to a country where they risk human rights violations such as arbitrary detention, torture or execution.

According to the legal adviser to the UN High Commissioner cited above, women may face particular problems in obtaining refugee status. A well-founded fear of persecution for reasons such as race, religion, political opinion, or membership of a particular social group is an internationally accepted standard for granting asylum. "Persecution of a woman will often take the form of sexual assault", stated the legal adviser. "Few women are able to discuss this experience with a male interviewer." Therefore, he continued, "where a woman has been persecuted (that is, subjected to such cruel, inhuman or degrading treatment as sexual assault), she finds it more difficult to establish her claim than a man".

The case of Catalina Mejía, a Salvadorian woman seeking asylum in the US illustrates a difficulty faced by some victims of sexual abuse. Throughout the 1980s, and into the 1990s, patterns of arbitrary arrest, torture, and killings have continued in El Salvador.

Rape and sexual humiliation committed by military personnel and police are among the methods of torture and ill-treatment reported. The Salvadorian Government has repeatedly failed to investigate claims of human rights abuses and to bring to justice those responsible.

Catalina Mejía worked as a dressmaker in a prov-

ince of El Salvador particularly affected by the 11-year-old conflict. She testified that during a search of her family's home by the military in 1983 a soldier ordered her outside at gunpoint, accused her and her family of being "guerrillas" (which they denied) and then raped her. During the next 18 months she was stopped twice at military checkpoints in other parts of El Salvador. At each checkpoint she was singled out by soldiers, who accused her of being a "guerrilla"; they let her go only after people waiting at the checkpoint, who knew her, intervened. She fled to the US in 1985. Still traumatized by her experience, she was unable to explain all that had happened to her to the male lawyer who first assisted her. She was, however, later able to confide in a female attorney, receive counselling, and testify about her experience.

The immigration judge presiding at her deportation hearing denied Catalina Mejía's application for political asylum in August 1988. The judge stated in her decision that "I have listened carefully to her lengthy testimony and observed her demeanour, and I find her to be altogether credible". But the judge concluded that Catalina Mejía had failed to establish "that she fears for her life or freedom, if deported to El Salvador". One of the reasons given by the judge for this decision was that the rape of Catalina Mejía by soldier who accused her of being a "guerrilla" was not an act of persecution but "was more because she was a female convenient to a brutal soldier acting only in his own self-interest". Catalina Mejía's appeal against the decision, to the US Board of Immigration Appeals, was pending in December 1990. Amnesty International has submitted a legal brief to the Board of Immigration Appeals, stating why Catalina Mejía would be at risk of human rights violations if returned to El Salvador. In its brief Amnesty International made the point that the immigration judge had erred in dismissing the rape as an act of self-interest. Rape in the circumstances described by Catalina Mejía amounts to torture, as defined in the UN Convention against Torture: any act by which severe pain or suffering, whether physical or mental, is intentionally inflicted by any government agent for "such purposes as... punishing... or intimidating... ".

Large numbers of refugees have fled to the US from Haiti, where widespread abuses by both Haitian Government agents and groups of armed civilians have been well documented. A Haitian woman refugee testified before an immigration judge in

1988 that armed men had abducted her husband and had assaulted her so severely that she miscarried and required hospital treatment. Yet the judge replied after hearing her case, "I still don't understand, even with all that, why [you felt] you had to leave your country." He denied her asylum claim. Information about the fate of her husband was not available at the time.

Refugees also may be at risk of abuses when confined in detention centres or camps in the country of refuge prior to determination of their status. Reported assaults on a number of Vietnamese women seeking asylum in Hong Kong reflect the victims' precarious situation. A Hong Kong police officer allegedly kicked and beat a woman, weighing only 38 kilos (84 pounds), at the Stonecutters Island Detention Centre in October 1989. She held a Vietnamese nursing certificate and was working at the detention centre to provide medical assistance for people who, like herself, sought asylum in Hong Kong.

When she attempted to retrieve a plastic rubbish bag for protection against the rain, she said, a police officer grabbed her hair and hit her with his baton. Then he kicked her in the stomach. When he struck her on the temple, she lost consciousness. A subsequent medical examination corroborated her allegations.

More than 100 Vietnamese men and women seeking asylum were apparently injured during indiscriminate assaults in July 1989, when Hong Kong police searched detainees' tents at the Shek Kong centre. A 28-year-old woman, who was nine months pregnant, was among the asylum-seekers ordered to stand outside their tents. A police officer first pulled her hair, she said. "He was holding a baton, and I thought he was about to hit me in the stomach. I put my hand in front of me to protect myself, and he struck my elbow with his baton." He then swore at her, according to her testimony, and left. "I do not know why he hit me", she said.

Another woman assaulted the same night in July explained that she was attempting to protect her three-year-old child when police kicked her. A medical examination showed a bruise on the woman's upper arm, with the imprint of a boot sole clearly delineated by dirt on the corresponding sleeve of her shirt.

Assaults on asylum-seekers and intimidation of victims and witnesses continued throughout 1989 in Hong Kong detention centres administered by the police. In the wake of international media reports

and protests about the treatment of Vietnamese asylum-seekers in Hong Kong, conditions appeared to have improved by late 1990.

The Executive Committee of the UN High Commissioner for Refugees adopted a conclusion in October 1990 which urges states and UN bodies to promote measures for improving the protection of women. The steps recommended include: providing female interviewers in procedures to determine refugee status; issuing individual, rather than family, identity documents to refugee women; ensuring that resettlement programs make special provision for women at risk; and identifying and prosecuting people who have committed crimes against refugee women. The committee also asked the Office of the UN High Commissioner for Refugees to develop comprehensive guidelines for the protection of refugee women, considering such action to be a matter of urgency.

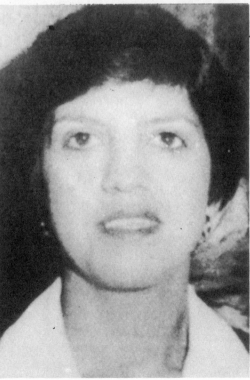

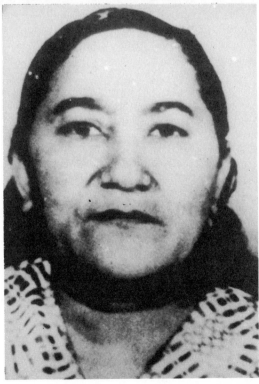

Vietnamese asylum-seekers (above) in detention on a ferry moored off Stonecutters Island, Hong Kong. Assaults on asylum-seekers in Hong Kong detention centres administered by the police were reported throughout 1989. More than 3,500 Colombians have been extrajudicially executed since mid-1987. They include members of the judiciary investigating human rights violations, such as María Elena Díaz Pérez (right), who was killed in July 1989 Margarida María Alves (far right), the leader of a rural workers trade union in the Brazilian state of Paraíba, was shot dead by gunmen in 1983. In 1987 lawyers working on another case of a "hired gun" killing found evidence that Margarida Alves had been killed by a death squad of military and civil police officers.

5

Twelve steps to protect women's human rights

Human rights for women, as for all individuals, are protected in international law. Yet women are among those imprisoned for their peaceful beliefs and activities, tortured, denied the right to a fair trial, abducted and "disappeared", and extrajudicially executed. Women also face human rights violations solely or primarily because of their sex.

Governments are responsible for upholding the international standards which safeguard the fundamental human rights of each and every one of their citizens. Yet governments often fail to take action to prevent human rights abuses.

The international community can play a decisive role in protecting human rights through vigilant and concerted action. Important steps towards protecting women's human rights worldwide include documenting human rights violations, publicizing these as widely as possible and campaigning to press government authorities for an end to the abuses. Governments which fail to protect fundamental human rights should be confronted with the force of international public opinion.

Amnesty International calls on all governments to implement the following 12-point program to protect women from human rights violations. The recommendations it contains address both the human rights violations which are primarily suffered by women, and the range of human rights abuses that women have experienced along with men and children. The campaign to protect women's human rights will have to be waged on the same fronts and the same issues as that to protect everyone's human rights. Some human rights violations, however, require specific action to protect women in particular. The recommendations below reflect the breadth of the campaign.

1 Stop rape, sexual abuse and other torture and ill-treatment by government agents

• Take effective steps to prevent the rape, sexual abuse and other torture and ill-treatment of detainees and prisoners.

• All law enforcement personnel should be instructed that these human rights violations will not be tolerated.

• Conduct prompt, thorough and impartial investigations into all reports of torture or ill-treatment. Any law enforcement agent responsible for such acts, or for encouraging or condoning them, should be brought to justice.

• Any form of detention or imprisonment and all measures affecting the human rights of detainees or prisoners should be subject to the effective control of a judicial authority.

- All detainees should be brought before a judge promptly after arrest.
- All detainees and prisoners should have access to family members and legal counsel promptly after arrest and regularly throughout their detention and/or imprisonment.
- The authorities should record the duration of any interrogation, the intervals between interrogations, and the identity of the officials conducting each interrogation and other persons present.
- Female guards should be present during the interrogation of female detainees and prisoners, and should be solely responsible for carrying out any body searches of female detainees and prisoners to reduce the risk of rape and other sexual abuses.
- Female detainees and prisoners should be held separately from male detainees and prisoners.
- Measures should be taken to prevent the opportunity for rape and sexual abuse, for example, by prohibiting contacts between male guards and female detainees and prisoners without the presence of a female guard.
- All female detainees and prisoners should be given the opportunity to have a medical examination promptly after admission to the place of custody and regularly thereafter. They should also have the right to be examined by a doctor of their choice.
- A medical examination, by a female doctor wherever possible, should be provided immediately for any female detainee or prisoner who alleges she has been raped. This is a crucial measure in obtaining evidence for legal prosecution.
- Victims of rape and sexual abuse by government agents, like all victims of torture and ill-treatment, should receive compensation and appropriate medical care.

2 Stop persecution because of family connections

- Any woman detained or imprisoned solely because of her family connections should be immediately and unconditionally released.
- The practice of torturing or ill-treating women in order to bring pressure on their relatives should not be tolerated. Anyone responsible for such acts should be brought to justice.
- The imprisonment of a mother and child together must never be used to inflict torture or ill-treatment on either by causing physical or mental suffering. If a child is ever separated from its mother in prison

she should be immediately notified and continuously kept informed of its whereabouts and given reasonable access to the child.

3 Provide adequate health care to all detainees and prisoners

- All detainees and prisoners must be provided with adequate medical treatment, denial of which can constitute ill-treatment.
- Provide all necessary pre-natal and post-natal care and treatment for women detainees and prisoners and their infants.
- Provide resources to treat conditions exclusively or primarily affecting women detainees and prisoners.

4 Release all prisoners of conscience immediately and unconditionally

- Release all prisoners of conscience, thousands of whom are women, detained or imprisoned because of their sex, beliefs, ethnic origin, language or religion, including those so detained for their peaceful participation in the political, social, economic or cultural life of their society.
- No woman should be detained or imprisoned for peacefully attempting to exercise basic rights and freedoms enjoyed by men.

5 Ensure prompt and fair trials for all political prisoners

- Stop unfair trials, which each year violate the fundamental rights of political prisoners in all parts of the world, including the rights of thousands of women.
- Ensure that all political prisoners charged with a criminal offence receive a prompt and fair trial by a competent, independent and impartial tribunal.
- Ensure that all political prisoners are treated in accordance with internationally recognized safeguards for fair legal proceedings, including the right to be informed at the time of arrest of the specific reasons for arrest; the right to challenge the legality of one's detention before a court; the right to be promptly informed of any charges; the right of anyone charged with a criminal offence to be presumed innocent, to have adequate time and facilities for the preparation of one's defence and to communicate with counsel of one's own choosing; the right to appeal one's conviction and sentence to a higher tribunal; the prohibition of invoking as evidence in any proceedings any statement made as a result of torture or ill-treatment (except against a person charged with perpetrating such mistreatment).

6 Take effective steps to prevent "disappearances"

- Stop "disappearances", which have affected thousands of women as victims and as relatives.
- Conduct prompt, thorough and impartial investigations into all reports of "disappearance" and bring to justice those responsible.
- Inform families immediately of any arrest and keep them informed of the whereabouts of the detainee or prisoner at all times.
- Detainees and prisoners should only be held in official, known detention centres, a list of which should be widely publicized.
- Women should never be subjected to human rights violations because of their search for a "disappeared" relative.
- Relatives of the "disappeared" should receive compensation.

7 Safeguard women's human rights in situations of armed conflict

- Uphold human rights in situations of armed conflict by stopping the imprisonment of prisoners of conscience, torture and ill-treatment, and extrajudicial executions, and by affording prompt and fair trials to all those detained for political reasons, in accordance with human rights guarantees and the norms of humanitarian law.

8 Prevent human rights violations against women refugees and asylum-seekers

- No woman, nor any other asylum-seeker, should be forcibly returned to a country where she can reasonably be expected to be imprisoned as a prisoner of conscience, tortured or executed.
- In procedures for the determination of refugee status governments should provide interviewers trained to recognize the specific protection needs of women refugees and asylum-seekers.
- Governments should thoroughly and impartially investigate human rights violations, including torture and ill-treatment, committed against refugee women and asylum-seekers in the country of asylum, and bring to justice those responsible.

9 Prevent human rights violations against women who are members of ethnic minorities

- Governments should recognize the special vulnerability of women who are members of ethnic minorities and indigenous populations and take urgent steps to protect them against human rights violations.

- Governments should publicly condemn and stop arbitrary detention, torture or ill-treatment, and extrajudicial execution of such women.
- Anyone responsible for such violations should be promptly brought to justice.

10 Stop judicial and extrajudicial executions. Abolish the death penalty

- Governments should abolish the death penalty and stop judicial and extrajudicial executions, practices which have deprived women, as well as men and children, of their most fundamental right — the right to life.
- All death sentences should be commuted.
- Thorough and speedy investigations should be conducted into suspected extrajudicial executions and those found responsible should be brought to justice.
- Forensic investigations into killings should be carried out promptly and thoroughly .
- Families and dependants of victims of extrajudicial executions should be given fair and adequate compensation.

11 Ratify international instruments for the protection of human rights

- Governments should ratify international legal instruments which provide for the protection of women's human rights, such as the International Covenant on Civil and Political Rights and its two Optional Protocols; the International Covenant on Economic, Social and Cultural Rights; the UN Convention against Torture and Other Cruel, Inhuman or Degrading Treatment or Punishment, and the Convention on the Elimination of All Forms of Discrimination against Women.

12 Support the work of relevant intergovernmental organizations

- Governments should publicly state their commitment to ensuring that the intergovernmental bodies which monitor violations of human rights suffered by women, including the UN Commission on the Status of Women and the Committee on the Elimination of Discrimination against Women, have adequate resources to carry out their task effectively.

Appendix 1

Protections provided by international standards

Amnesty International's 12-point program for the protection of women against human rights violations is based on internationally recognized human rights standards.

Recommendation 1: The Universal Declaration of Human Rights, the International Covenant on Civil and Political Rights (ICCPR) and the UN Convention against Torture prohibit all acts of torture and cruel, inhuman or degrading treatment or punishment. Practical safeguards for detainees and prisoners are provided in the Convention against Torture and in the UN Body of Principles for the Protection of All Persons under Any Form of Detention or Imprisonment.The UN Convention against Torture requires each State Party to "take effective legislative, administrative, judicial or other measures to prevent acts of torture in any territory under its jurisdiction".

Recommendation 2: In 1980 the UN Commission on Human Rights called upon governments to ensure that no one is denied basic rights because of their connection, "particularly family connection, with a suspect, an accused person, or a person who has been convicted". Detention solely because of one's family connection constitutes arbitrary detention.

Recommendation 3: Denying detainees adequate medical care can constitute ill-treatment. The UN Standard Minimum Rules for the Treatment of Prisoners stipulate that all prisoners must be provided with adequate medical services. In addition these UN Rules recognize the special needs of pregnant women and nursing mothers held in official custody and provide for "all necessary pre-natal and post-natal care and treatment".

Recommendation 4: The Universal Declaration of Human Rights and the ICCPR prohibit arbitrary detention and guarantee rights including freedom of conscience, expression, association and assembly.These international instruments also require that governments apply all the rights they contain to all individuals, without any discrimination of any kind including on the grounds of sex. The Convention on the Elimination of All Forms of Discrimination against Women, adopted by the UN in 1979, condemns discrimination against women, including "distinction, exclusion or restriction made on the basis of sex which has the effect or purpose of impairing or nullifying the recognition, enjoyment or exercise by women... of their human rights and fundamental freedoms".

Recommendation 5: International instruments, including the Universal Declaration of Human Rights and the ICCPR guarantee the right to a prompt, fair and public hearing by an independent and impartial tribunal. The specific internationally recognized requirements for legal proceedings are set forth in the ICCPR and other instruments, including the UN Basic Principles on the Independence of the Judiciary.

Recommendation 6: UN General Assembly Resolution 33/173 adopted in 1978 calls on governments "in the event of reports of enforced or involuntary disappearances, to devote appropriate resources to searching for such persons and to undertake speedy and impartial investigations". It also calls on governments "to ensure that law enforcement and security authorities or organizations are fully accountable, especially in law, in the discharge of their duties, such accountability to include legal responsibility for unjustifiable excesses which might lead to enforced and involuntary disappearances and to other violations of human rights". The UN

Working Group on Enforced or Involuntary Disappearances concluded in its 1990 report that "perhaps the single most important factor contributing to the phenomenon of disappearances may be that of impunity" and that "perpetrators of human rights violations, whether civilian or military, will become all the more brazen when they are not held to account before a court of law." UN bodies have also stressed the right of families of the "disappeared" to know the fate of their relatives.

Recommendation 7: In times of armed conflict not only do human rights norms apply, but also humanitarian law, including the 1949 Geneva Conventions and their Protocols I and II. Article 3 in each of the 1949 Geneva Conventions recognizes the particular risks faced by civilians in situations of internal civil turmoil and armed conflict. This Article prohibits, with regard to non-combatants, "violence to life and person, in particular murder of all kinds, mutilation, cruel treatment and torture". It also prohibits "outrages upon personal dignity, in particular humiliating and degrading treatment". Among the guarantees provided by Protocol I to the Geneva Conventions, addressing international armed conflict, is protection against rape, forced prostitution, and other forms of sexual assault.

Recommendation 8: The Universal Declaration of Human Rights specifies that "everyone has the right to seek and to enjoy in other countries asylum from persecution".

The principle of *non-refoulement*, set out in Article 33 of the 1951 UN Convention relating to the Status of Refugees, prohibits the return of refugees and asylum-seekers to any territory where their life or freedom would be threatened on account of their race, religion, nation-

ality, membership of a particular social group, or political opinion. The principle of *non-refoulement* is recognized by the international community as a norm of general international law, binding on all states, irrespective of whether they are party to the 1951 Convention.

The Executive Committee of the UN High Commissioner for Refugees in October 1990 urged states and UN bodies to promote measures for improving the protection of women refugees.

Recommendation 9: Many women who are members of ethnic minorities have suffered arbitrary detention, torture or ill-treatment, and extrajudicial execution, solely because of their origins. The Universal Declaration of Human Rights and subsequent international agreements provide protection against such abuses for all women, men, and children.

Recommendation 10: The Universal Declaration of Human Rights recognizes each person's right to life and categorically states that no one shall be subjected to torture or to cruel, inhuman or degrading treatment or punishment. Amnesty International believes that the death penalty is the extreme form of cruel, inhuman or degrading punishment and violates the right to life.

The Second Optional Protocol to the ICCPR, adopted by the UN General Assembly in December 1989, is the world's first treaty of universal scope which gives governments the opportunity to commit themselves to stopping executions and abolishing the death penalty.

Specific measures aimed at stopping extrajudicial executions are set forth in the UN Principles on the Effective Prevention and Investigation of Extra-Legal, Arbitrary and Summary Executions. The Principles require governments to prohibit

extrajudicial executions, whatever the circumstances they face.

Recommendation 11: By ratifying international conventions protecting human rights a government affirms to the international community its determination to respect the dignity and value of each of its citizens. UN Secretary-General Javier Pérez de Cuéllar stated that ratifying the International Covenants on Human Rights "is one of the most concrete demonstrations a state can make of its commitment to human rights". In repeated resolutions the UN General Assembly has urged all states that have not yet done so to become party to the International Covenants, the Convention against Torture and the Convention on the Elimination of All Forms of Discrimination against Women. The UN General Assembly has also urged all member states of the UN to accord priority to the dissemination of the Universal Declaration of Human Rights, the International Covenants on Human Rights and other international human rights instruments in their respective national and local languages and to make them known as widely as possible in their territories.

Recommendation 12: The UN General Assembly, in resolutions adopted relating to the human rights of women, has recognized the important contribution to the protection of the human rights of women by UN bodies such as the Commission on the Status of Women and the Committee on the Elimination of Discrimination against Women.

Women in the Front Line

Subject Index

Names in the Report

Fatima Abbas (Syria) 4,5
Samiha Abdel-Hamid (Egypt) 7
Hawa Abdillahi (Somalia) 46
Jihad 'Abs (Syria) 29
Mohamed Lamine ould Ahmed (W.Sahara) 14
Na'ila 'A'esh (Israel/OT) 24
Martha Angula (Namibia) 9
Susan Aniban (Philippines) 4
Vicky Ashikoto (Namibia) 9
Margarida Maria Alves (Brazil) 13,51
Gunta Behn (India) 19
Alita Bona (Philippines) 14
Velma Barfield (US) 34
Sanasam Ongbi Belu (India) 10,39
Fatma Abu Bakra (Israel/OT) 23
Nezha al-Bernoussi (Morocco) 12
Kahindo Bozelo (Zaire) 14
Terry Boulatta (Israel/OT) 28
Nurten Caglar (Turkey) 9
Doina Cornea (Romania) 8,11
Anna Chertkova (USSR) 27
Berrin Ceylan (Turkey) 27
Anna Ciherean (Romania) 20
Maria Morales Caro (Colombia)39
Cheng Mingxia (China) 41
Rinzen Choeny (Tibetan Autonomous Region) 13
Fatima Chenna (Morocco)14,17
Sara Christina Chan Chan Medina 19,35
Phyllis Coard (Grenada) 27
Paula Cooper (USA) 34
Guadalupe Ccallocanto (Peru) 45
Rula Abu Dahu (Israel/OT) 23
Buthina Dowka (Sudan) 9
Dan Jing (China) 41
"Deepika" (Sri Lanka) 38
Tahani Sulayman Abu Daqqa (Israel/OT) 12
Maria Elena Diaz Perez (Colombia)10,51
Ongbi Bino Devi (India) 39
Carmen Ferro Estrada (Peru) 30
Widjan Faris (Israel/OT) 27
Mairead Farrell (UK) 42,48
Miriam Firouz (Iran)
Valdeta Fejzullai (Yugoslavia) 30
Dona Maria de Guia (Brazil) 17
Consuelo Garcia Santa Cruz (Peru) 12
Rosario Godoy de Cuevas (Guatemala)3,5
Maria Cristina Gomez (El Salvador) 12-3
May al-Hafez (Syria) 28
Makkiyya 'Abdullah Hamdam (Saudi Arabia) 33
Embarca ment Taleb ould Husein (Western Sahara) 10
Namat Issa (Ethiopia) 30
Fahima Dahir Jama (Somalia) 33
Gurmeet Kaur (India) 6,28
Kim Young-ae (South Korea) 24
Malika Khalufi (Syria) 14

Rafat Kholdi (Iran) 22
Seviye Kopru (Turkey) 5,33
Solema Jubilan (Philippines) 10
Salka ment Najem ould Omar Lahsen (Western Sahara) 35
Sebbaha ment Mohamed ould Lehbib (Western Sahara) 35
Angelina Llenaresas (Philippines) 35
Li Xiuping (China) 12
Long Xiangping (China) 9,25
Cristano Losande (Philippines)
Edna Losande (Philippines) 46
Elsa "Tita" Lubi (Philippines) 23
Ma Ziyi (China) 41
Soledad Mabilangan (Philippines) 14
Safia Hashi Madar (Somalia) 5,9
Samira Hassan Mahdi (Sudan(32
Sophie Mahlaelu (South Africa) 25
Sara al-Fadil Mahmoud (Sudan) 11,13
Pamela Majodina (South Africa)28
Deborah "Debs" Josephine Marakalla (South Africa) 12,16
Juan Francisco Massi Chavez (El Salvador) 35
Fatuma Mbholu (Zaire) 14
Maria Juana Medina (El Salvador) 19
Dhabia Khemis Mehairi (UAE) 9,11
Catalina Mejia (El Salvador) 49
Angelica Mendoza de Ascarza (Peru) 25
Noma India Mfeketo (South Africa) 4
Veliswa Mhlawuli (South Africa) 9-10
Nineth Montenegro de Garcia (Guatemala) 3
Wafa' Murtada (Syria) 24
Chamani Muthuhetti (Sri Lanka) 38
Griffiths Mxenge (S.Africa) 38
Nonyamezelo Victoria Mxenge (South Africa) 38
Zahra' Habib Mansur al-Nasser (Saudia Arabia) 13.16
Marilyn Negro (Philippines) 46
Sara Abdullah Nugdullah (Sudan) 14
Cecilia Olea (Peru) 12
Gonul Ortakci (Turkey) 8
Fatima Chenna Oufkir (Morocco) 14
General Mohamed Oufkir (Morocco) 14
Fatma Ozyurt (Turkey) 27
Josepha Padcayan (Philippines) 46
Hugo Paner (Philippines) 15
Jose Rolando Pantaleon (Guatemala) 14
Dr.Alirio de Jesus Pedraza Becerra (Colombia) 25
Patricia Pena (Chile) 24
Ana Maria Carmen del Perez (Argentina) 35
Rosie Paner (Philippines) 15
Maria Guinarita Pisco Pisango (Peru) 21
Hind Qahwaji (Syria) 10
Amal 'Abd al-Wahad Qasisa (Israel/OT) 25
Husniyya 'Abd al-Qader (Israel/OT) 26,33
Theresa Ramashamole (South Africa) 21,32
Consuelo Hernandez Ramirez (Guatemala) 14
Celina Ramos (El Salvador) 8
Elba Julia Ramos (El Salvador) 8
Carole Richardson (UK) 20-21,32
Martina Shanahan (UK)27